The New Stone Age

THE New Stone Age

Ideas & Inspiration for Living with Crystals

CAROL WOOLTON

Photographs by Jon Day

TEN SPEED PRESS
California | New York

FOR  Genevieve & Eleanor

contents

CLEAR ——————————— Rock Crystal 25

Increasing clarity to recover from burnout

YELLOW ——————————— Citrine 41

Fostering creativity to overcome indecisiveness

ORANGE ——————————— Carnelian 55

Empowering action to release old hurts

PINK ——————————— Rose Quartz 69

Nurturing love and compassion to increase connectedness

RAINBOW ——————————— Agate 83

Learning patience and persistence to reduce restlessness

PURPLE ——————————— Amethyst 97

Gaining calm and lucidity to resist dependency

RED ——————————— Garnet 113

Improving grounding and stability to minimize anxiety

Introduction

The color of every crystal is unique, depending on its individual journey and the environment in which it was formed. Most are found buried in the earth's crust or in gravel weathered away from larger rocks. Nature's upheavals are responsible: vast geological shifts, volcanic eruptions, the sinking of continents, and erosion of mountains give these crystal survivors an aura of magic. Time is important. When molten rock cools quickly, tiny crystals form. A slower cooling, combined with enough space inside of hollows and cavities, allows larger crystals to grow.

We describe crystals as growing, because over time they do. They branch and spike, in what appear like subterranean gardens, as more atoms connect with each other in orderly repeated geometric patterns. This perfect symmetry mimics nature's other phenomena, such as snowflakes, the whorls of a petal, or a butterfly's wings. At the same time, their colors remind us of the beauty of nature and that something bigger and stronger exists beyond us. People talk of them as being alive, because their inner color can alter, appearing to fire up or fade depending on the light and time of day. Even weather patterns can effect changes, making a crystal appear almost animated.

Over the centuries, the shiny geometric structure of crystals has accrued a unique combination of history, geological knowledge, and spiritual properties. The latter are being rediscovered to help with today's challenges. It seems ironic that as contemporary life advances at a quickened pace, collectively, we are emulating the behavior of ancient cultures, seeking the reassuring sense of permanence and natural beauty that a crystal, with its deep connection to Mother Earth, can provide. In spite of living in an exciting era of innovation, with limitless technology and information at our fingertips, the changing social, economic, and political climates feel like a gathering storm propelling us to use these stones—as our ancient ancestors did—as a purposeful shield for daily life.

OPPOSITE Black tourmaline in a weathered wooden bowl by Anna Unwin at Aubespoke Studio

What is the difference between a mineral and a crystal? Broadly speaking, a *mineral* is a naturally formed inorganic solid, stable at room temperature, with a characteristic chemical composition and crystalline structure. Typically, a mineral is identified by its color, luster, cleavage, fracture, and crystal form. A *crystal* is a natural solid composed of atoms, molecules, and ions arranged in a highly ordered and precise microscopic structure forming a crystal lattice of regular geometric repeated patterns. All minerals produce crystals, and minerals may be referred to as rocks or stones. Roughly, there are three thousand minerals, but only two hundred are used as gemstones, in a cut and polished form, and set into jewelry. There are many technicalities in the world of mineralogy that I won't delve into; for instance, lapis lazuli, unlike other crystal and gem materials, contains multiple minerals, so it is actually labeled a rock. As the distinctions are not relevant to our purposes, this book uses the terms *mineral* and *crystal,* interchangeably.

Many millennials have rejected their forebears' practice of wearing jewels as status symbols. Ornamentation for this generation is more personal rather than a type of symbolism to proclaim their particular group or tribe. The era of "fake news," insecurity induced by social media, ill-paid employment, and expensive housing has made crystals a comforting touchstone they can trust. Young people share crystal obsessions in a quasi-religious way on Instagram and create sleek crystal glossary apps to download and use as a meditation.

The stones have a connection with the earth that provides comfort and purpose, fulfilling a human desire for something meaningful beyond the self. The realization of the effects of human behavior on the environment is powering a global objective to save the planet along with new appreciation of the physical treasures the earth produces.

Created eons ago, crystals represent a grander intention of honoring the earth, as well as promoting our own small, private goals. There is a moral value, too, in eschewing a synthetic man-made material in favor of crystal. It's a battle of our times, lending a young crystal-wearing generation the air of warriors as they struggle to change behavior toward the earth.

> "For a great many people, a single gemstone alone is enough to provide the highest and most perfect aesthetic experience of the wonders of nature."
>
> —PLINY THE ELDER, *NATURALIS HISTORIA*

"Relationships, isolation, financial security, rootlessness, personal safety, and trust—all of these are really creating pressure," says hypnotherapist Elizabeth Hearn, counting on her fingers a few of the major stress triggers for women today. Adding to those, she cites "women's high expectations of themselves."

As much as technology has benefited women's lives as a connective force for good, Hearn warns, "it makes us far more vulnerable in terms of who we can trust." We are also wrestling with social constructs that women didn't have to worry about thirty or so years ago: anxiety induced by a child addicted to the internet; eating disorders; overwhelming consumerism; and the strange truth that social media appears to have become our gatekeeper. In this untrusting climate, ancient rituals are springing up as a means of restoring a state of resilience, inner balance, and stability as the pace of change quickens all around us. Crystals have become a portable safety net for the new Stone Age.

"I don't see it as woo-woo or mysterious," says Hearn, who in the 1980s started using crystals that she sourced in New York's West Village. "I see it as something that's really sustainable. And for a person to be able to identify what speaks to them in terms of stones is really useful." Hearn believes wearing a stone has a cumulative effect. "Over weeks and months, you can have a new default response, instead of a stressed or panicked one," she says. "It can help you become more mindful."

In ancient Egyptian culture, honoring the feminine was an important principle—one we are now looking back to emulate. "The inclusion and elevation of women correlate with the signs of a healthy society," writes philanthropist Melinda Gates in her 2019 book, *The Moment of Lift: How Empowering Women Changes the World*. Goddesses were held in every bit as much esteem as male gods, and the high status of females is visible in the cultural artifacts they left behind. Women and girls in the developed world may be healthier, better educated, and more autonomous than in any previous age but our fight for equality isn't over. We have a new set of complex issues to deal with that have no equivalent in the past.

The ancients used stones to activate their consciousness—to feel the full capacity of their senses in order to navigate their "earth experience" and perceive realms beyond death. Some Egyptologists believe the ancients' search for enlightenment gave them a heightened sense of perception—in the same way we visit the gym, they exercised their "sense muscles" on a daily basis, using stones and crystals to learn to live well, with a lighter heart.

Four thousand years ago, the ancient Egyptians mined crystals in valleys east of the Nile to satisfy their demand for colorful stones such as malachite, garnet, hematite, turquoise, and carnelian, which they were convinced were beneficial. They trusted that placing crystals on the body would release a healing energy onto wounds and attributed a practical purpose to each stone. Night terrors? Topaz was the cure. Carnelian purified the blood. Small amulets of red jasper treated infertility. Malachite was crushed into an alluring green kohl, which shaded and protected the eyes. Turquoise was popular as a sign of joy. Lapis lazuli, imported from Afghanistan, was reminiscent of the heavens, creation, and rebirth. The intense blue stone would be ground and rubbed into the crown of the head to draw out spiritual impurities. Much later, Cleopatra used emeralds mined near the Red Sea and rose quartz in a bid for eternal youth.

Ancient Egyptians equated the process of refining a crystal to spiritual purification. When a stone was cut and the rough exterior removed, its gleaming soul was revealed. We can only imagine the heart-lurching chemical reaction experienced by the first person to stumble across a crystal glinting from the soil, a piece of magic borne from the earth's crust. Under those circumstances, believing the stone to have sacred powers would have been inevitable. It would have been only a small step to believe one could harness this power by adorning oneself with it.

The belief that crystals are silent protectors, capable of sustaining their daily life, echoes down the centuries in a way that is relevant for modern life. The ancients had a profound connection to nature—which our city-led civilization has lost, to our collective detriment—that can be regained in the depths of a crystal.

In 2019, at the World Economic Forum in Davos, Switzerland, naturalist Sir David Attenborough told an audience of business leaders, politicians, and other delegates, "I was born during the Holocene—the twelve-thousand-year period of climatic stability that allowed humans to settle, farm, and create civilizations." This led to trade in ideas and goods, and eventually made us a globally connected species. Now, we're entering a new geologic age, the Anthropocene. It's the age of human-produced changes as well as other climactic changes that have damaged the earth—and therefore, as Attenborough then pointed out, ourselves. Crystals and stone, which were one of the first goods traded, linked the ancients to others as well as to the earth, and they can reignite this purpose in our contemporary hearts and minds.

The desire for ritual endures. Every human from birth shares a common quest for meaning, and repeated patterns of behavior can be important for our security, comfort, and sense of belonging.

I can't fully explain the energy of a crystal itself, but I can explain certain emotions that people experience as they come to think of themselves in new ways. You could argue that the inexplicable happenings I and others have witnessed around crystals are simply a case of chance and coincidence, but nonetheless they were real experiences. The aim of a crystal is to foster a deeper feeling of happiness and fulfillment. There's no scientific double-blind experiment that can testify to that, but we do have the "case study" results of life trajectories that have changed for the better—some of which are included in the chapters that follow.

Sadly, crystals aren't magic spells. There are no miracles or "cures." You can't tuck a rose quartz, known as the supporter of all forms of love, underneath your pillow to guarantee finding *the* one. But working closely with a stone, and charging it with your intentions, can lead to balance and mental clarity. Your ability to determine what sparks joy in life might be sharpened, and you might find yourself considering what matters most, which will include relationships. The quartz can help illuminate what you need to discard, as you gradually clear out old toxic emotions to help yourself sleep better.

Everyone can tap in to crystal power. And this renewed faith in crystals is gaining momentum as we collectively seek an improved rhythm of life and define what it means to be a modern human being. There is but one single rule: you need to work earnestly with your crystal. Life improvements can happen, but as with all relationships, it works best when you make a commitment. There might not be just one stone that's perfect for you. Like me, you might require different crystals at different moments. Think of this book as part of your rainbow tool kit for better living, because the ultimate goal of using any crystal is to feel free.

Crystal Intervention

A grand Victorian wood display case in London's Natural History Museum houses a couple of pea-size beads found at Es-Skhul, a prehistoric cave in Israel. At first glance, you would walk straight past, as there seems to be nothing special about the beads at all; I've seen zillions of other more striking, colorful, or otherwise notable beads. The remarkable thing about them is their age. The chemical analysis of the sediment stuck to them shows that they came from layers of earth dating back to 100,000 years ago. These beads are the earliest known piece of jewelry.

Imagine the world in which this decorated antecedent would have been living. In my mind, I see the girl with the bead necklace, and I visualize the monumental differences between her daily routines and ours, in whom she loved, and what would have frightened or excited her. I wonder what fears and anxieties kept her awake at night. She would have experienced the burdens of hunger, disease, childbirth, and dangerous predators.

Looking closer at the beads, you can see the small holes deliberately perforated with a sharp flint tool that allowed them to be strung together into a necklace. The owner wore the beads to send a message—maybe that she was powerful or that she was part of a certain tribe—as well as to function as a protector and guardian over her.

We share this girl's DNA, passed through the centuries, as well as the primal human desire to adorn and decorate. What strikes me as a new phenomenon is how the increasingly fast pace and global uncertainty of twenty-first-century life is driving us to return to the roots of her symbolic behavior, first practiced eons ago on the slopes of Mount Carmel.

A stone jewel allows us to look beyond our own lives; each unknowing sliver forms a bridge linking us to the experience of our forebears. Ancient superstitions survive in a myriad of Irish shamrocks, guardian serpents, and evil eyes, as well as golden horns, which were originally placed on walls of buildings for protection in the Neolithic period. Every so often a trendy new scarab surfaces on a piece of jewelry, though the symbol was first worn four thousand years ago by ancient Egyptians, who associated the scarab beetle with wisdom, renewal, and protection from death. Most early forms of jewelry were designed to bring the owner good luck or to ward off malevolent influences.

OPPOSITE A back-lit cathedral-point smoky quartz raised on a plinth picks up glints of gold highlighted by the pyrite lying alongside

A complex web of history, symbolism, and tradition is woven into the stones of the charms and talismans that we wear—though we are often unaware of their mythological origins or, in certain cases, the once-powerful religious role they played. But the belief in the symbolic power of a talisman is universal. Millions of people around the world in different cultures carry something each day: a string of prayer beads rattling in a pocket, a "knock on wood" ankh, a turquoise hand of Fatima, or a simple golden wishbone or mossy-green crystal four-leaf clover dangling from a chain.

> "That we find a crystal or a poppy beautiful means that we are less alone, that we are more deeply inserted into existence than the course of a single life would lead us to believe."
>
> —JOHN BERGER

The Now Age

This Stone Age sensibility is resonating with the now-age fashion crowd and beyond. At the Natural History Museum, I noticed people meditating in front of a case holding a rare piece of painite, a mesmerizing purple and dark pink stone from Myanmar. Out on the street, I spotted discs of sliced agate and rough nuggets of crystal on pendants glinting beneath shirts of both sexes as they passed by—and, no doubt, secreted in their bags and rucksacks were pebbles of shungite crystal, to reduce radiation from their mobile phones.

Back in my office at *Vogue*, I noticed that the beauty director's desk was littered with blue celestite and tiger's-eye; she is working on an article about Miranda Kerr's line of organic products, which are filtered through rose quartz. Other modern beauty therapists, convinced of crystals' benefits for the skin, are incorporating them into masks and face creams, oils and bath rituals, to clear out impurities.

Many Hollywood actresses and celebrities keep crystals close by at all times. One (who has sworn me to secrecy) keeps a lozenge of citrine in her bra all day. She's joined the growing group of celebrity crystal lovers who, in their determination to collect the best specimens, have found themselves a dealer.

I recently asked model and businesswoman Kate Moss what her favorite stone is at the moment. "I'm not going to tell you," she answers protectively, "otherwise everyone will try and buy some." She wears a leather necklace with seven diamonds facing the front, and five amethysts on the inside, touching the skin, for protection. "It's an amulet," Moss explains, "which brings good energy that has meaning and you can wear it every day." Although garnet is her birthstone, she often turns to amethysts. "I find them more organic; I feel they're a bit more spiritual. There's something earthy about them."

Wooden box of crystal shards prepped for an Amaryllis Fraser artwork

Fashion designer, businesswoman, and performer Victoria Beckham surrounds herself with rose quartz and black tourmaline backstage before her fashion shows. "If I told you my backstage rituals, and was honest, you would think I was a little weird. I carry crystals with me," she confesses, "which some people might think as odd, but it works for us." Beckham is part of the new movement whose adherents ascribe a mystical power to crystal. Kendall Jenner and Kim Kardashian, of the reality TV show *Keeping Up with the Kardashians* and its spin-offs, are both self-professed crystal enthusiasts. Kim Kardashian released a perfume line called "KKW Crystal" that is bottled in a quartz-shaped case and arrives in a bed of crystals. Gwyneth Paltrow's lifestyle site, Goop, extols the virtues of stones, offering starter kits of eight crystals for medicine bags, crystal therapy lectures at a health summit, and stone eggs for yoni health (but more about that later).

Singer Adele attributed a stellar 2016 show at London's O2 arena to her crystals. Then came a performance of which she was less proud. "The worst, most disastrous performance," she claimed in an interview, was when, "the Grammys came and I lost my f-ing crystals."

I have a friend who sleeps like a baby underneath a crystal canopy, and actress Zoë Kravitz visits Brooklyn-based healer Kalisa Augustine for energy-clearing sessions during which she lies on a crystal bed.

For a recent show, Italian fashion designer Riccardo Tisci paired geode slip dresses with discs of agate, and Britain's Cottweiler menswear designers staged a show in front of the painite stone in the crystal room at the Natural History Museum, right where I spotted the meditation taking place. Glamorous designers such as Noor Fares and Eugenie Niarchos visit Arizona's gemstone fair, bringing back agate and crystal to give their collections a modern mystical vibe.

What works on the catwalk can also manifest itself in other spaces. The concept that a well-placed crystal can heal the home as well as improve the function and flow of energy is pervasive. Crystal grids are being laid beneath workout studios—amethyst, quartz, and rose quartz in the center for calming and support, with black tourmaline and pyrite around the perimeter to block negative energy. Teams of "crystal cleaners," a sophisticated cross between feng shui experts and house doctors, will visit and prescribe particular stones

ABOVE A collection of rare minerals, crystals, taxidermy, coral, silver shells, jewelry, and curiosities arranged at Creel and Gow in NYC

to clear up the energy flow. But these geological curios and crystal specimens with their extraordinary colors and shapes are also forming part of carefully curated collections for art lovers. They are lit and displayed on pedestals by the interior designers for Wall Street entrepreneurs, Silicon Valley billionaires, and film stars who are willing to pay tens of thousands of dollars to display these specimens as decorative artworks.

"Mobile phones are the reason we're so busy, because none of us can shut off like we did before," Charlotte Tilbury—makeup and skincare authority and founder of her eponymous brand—tells me at the end of an exhausting day as she's preparing supper for her young son. "And the irony is that they're run on crystals." It feels natural for Tilbury to have rock crystal, rose quartz, and amethyst around the house, because she grew up on the Spanish island of Ibiza with bohemian parents who believed in crystals' healing powers. "Time is so speeded up that we need an antidote to calm down. I play a crystal bowl, which has a sound like an alien angel and puts me into a deep meditative state. The world has never needed more healing or to get in touch with nature more than now."

Tilbury travels constantly, taking the bowl, which she calls her "little friend," with her for meditation. She finds it helpful for creative visualizations. "Your intention has to be clear," she advises. "Crystals can amplify all your thoughts, and you are what you think." She likens the effect of crystals to makeup, which also brings joy and makes a woman the most confident version of herself. "People judge themselves so much, and makeup isn't about hiding; it's about enhancing. If you look back in time, whether it's Cleopatra or someone donning war paint, we've always used it."

At age sixteen, Tilbury knew makeup would be her purpose in life. "If you believe something, it will become your reality. Crystals were a fast track to what I wanted to do—then I spent years honing it," she says. Technology is embedded in every area of our life, along with its capacity to stress. The remedy, in Tilbury's opinion, is the ability of the light and energy of crystals to spread joy and calm.

Light & Energy

As we will see later, crystals are natural conductors of energy—but why would that affect our own vitality? From a scientific perspective, it necessarily follows; the vibratory frequency theory for healing is unproven. Yet many believe that crystals produce a friction that can influence the energy of those in contact with it.

Our energy is promoted by our sense of sight and touch. Primarily what draws us to a crystal is light, manifesting itself as color, which like other electromagnetic waves is measurable. Light is dispersed, refracted, and distributed around a stone, even when it's not transparent. Shine a flashlight beneath a cloudy piece of selenite, and the channel of light travels straight up, shining like a beacon. Brilliant-cut diamonds are still faceted based on master cutter Marcel Tolkowsky's mathematical calculations from 1919. His guidelines create the perfect proportions to reflect the most light from the top of the stone.

The temperature of a stone changes and reacts when heat is transferred from our hands, and as heat is also a form of energy, it too can be measured. Gemstone expert Robert Procop—who draws on inspirations from actress and humanitarian Angelina Jolie to create Style of Jolie jewels, which funds schools in conflict areas—tested the temperature of a pale pink kunzite in his Beverly Hills office before and after I held it. He used a temperature-difference sensor, placing the probe tip against the kunzite, so we could detect how quickly the surface temperature rose within five seconds. "Every single element is measurable by electricity," Procop insists. "We generate energy from friction given by an outside source, which is why we can get static shocks touching surfaces. As soon as you put a test into a stone, it will generate a conductive property."

Thermal properties and light are proven stimulants to us, and stones are also known to react to elements within our environment. However, this leaves a remaining unknown that can't be tested: the emotional reaction of whoever holds a stone and its particular synergy with that person—both of which can vary wildly. It's personal. There is no right or wrong interpretation of a crystal; it takes time and practice to recognize any subtle sensations that you feel. One might give you a sense of calm while another might foster a sense of motivation and energy.

Anything that inspires hope in us, whether that is a person, event, or crystal, sparks a positive response. Conversely, because thought is an invisible energy that shapes our mind, and our relationship, to the world, the consequences of negative thinking are equally influential on our lives. The energy a crystal transfers, in Procop's experience, tips the scales in life toward acceptance and positivity. They are the small stones upon which you construct a better narrative and brighter outlook

"Crystals are a life force," explains Procop, "whether it's a rough or faceted stone, [what] you're holding there is a transference of positivity and confidence." The message is simple: the stone can change your energy, which in turn can change your life.

———

Most scientists believe the power of a crystal is merely the power of suggestion working on the human mind—what's called a placebo effect. Like beauty, though, power can be in the eye of the beholder. If someone is firmly convinced that a stone produces certain results, this conviction will impress itself upon her thoughts—and following that, her body. Belief itself

can shift psychology. The results can manifest themselves as powerfully as if vibrations from the body of the stone caused them.

The placebo effect has long been recognized. In 1807, Thomas Jefferson wrote to a friend, "One of the most successful physicians I have ever known assured me that he used more bread pills, drops of colored water, and powders of hickory ashes, than of all the other medicines put together."

Ted Kaptchuk, a professor of medicine at Harvard Medical School and a leading figure in placebo studies, seems to concur with Jefferson's doctor friend. "Placebo has generally been denigrated in medicine, but I always wanted to figure out ways to ethically harness it," Kaptchuk wrote, suggesting its therapeutic actions can be genuine and robust, and that placebo-induced benefits should be promoted, not dismissed.

In a bid to link age-old thinking about crystals with quantum physics, integrated health physician and doctor of Chinese medicine Stefan Chmelik is developing a wearable piece of tech that looks like a smooth pebble studded with crystal. Meant to work in tandem with a smartphone to control stress, the Sensate device vibrates with low frequency sound waves to affect the vagus nerve lying beneath the breastbone. This nerve holds the key to keeping calm, as it runs from the brain to the gut, touching every major organ on the way. It controls the rapid breath, increased heart rate, and raised blood pressure of the fight-or-flight response. The Sensate pulses on the nerve in time to calming music downloaded from the app and channeled through earphones.

Chmelik is seeing positive health benefits. When I visited his clinic, he told me, "In evolutionary biology, the first thing that developed was our sense of vibration, so we could detect an approaching threat or a mate. We've received these vibrations over millions of years, so the power of a stone makes sense. It can help control stress resiliency and trigger relaxation responses."

With Chmelik's device, crystals, particularly his favorite stone fluorite, have a double-whammy calming effect. I'd come to try out Sensate, so Chmelik checked my stress biomarker rates, and I chose a device with citrine that I clipped onto my bra, down toward my solar plexus (just like my actress friend).

"Our instinct level is so intense," he said, "but it's that of a 500-million-year-old reptile, which goes into flight, fright, or freeze mode." The problem, he explained, is that the brain stem is powerful, but not smart, so it can't differentiate between real and imagined threat. No human being has lived under the type of stress that people are now experiencing in developed countries. We're not stressed about having a roof over our heads any longer—it's about work deadlines and home commitments. The result is that your brain can't distinguish between physiological and psychological threats, and it has only one response: to release adrenaline. This means it applies the same life-or-death response to almost anything. Even something as simple such as too many emails could be perceived as a physical danger.

OPPOSITE An assortment of soothing crystals used by Place 8 Healing in Los Angeles

After only ten minutes with the device, my stats and busy mind have improved; however, as Chmelik pointed out, statistics can't change behavior. It's how you feel that makes the difference. I feel relaxed, with a clear mind, and I don't particularly want the experiment to end.

"In my view, stress resiliency will be the single most useful skill of the twenty-first century to change health-risk profiles and enable adaptability," he says. The Sensate can be programmed to switch on automatically when stress levels increase; on the other hand, crystals are fully charged and work 24/7. In a world where people feel overwhelmed or overworked, vibrational energy could be described as a magic bullet in terms of well-being. In which case, scientific proof or not, if a crystal believer's vagus nerve is strengthened, the user will cope with stress more effectively and become calmer. And that has a proven health benefit.

Color & Energy

Color can be an important contributor to the placebo effect. In tests, people responded better to blue pills as sedatives and white pills for pain relief. This shows that the ability to feel better is rooted in an individual's own beliefs and expectations, so even if a crystal is used as a figurative reminder of that intention, its results can be significant, and its color plays a part.

In Greece, around the fifth century BCE, Hippocrates, the father of modern Western medicine, became the first color theorist to link color with well-being. He observed certain shared character traits of four personality types and their behavior patterns. He believed it was possible to determine the physiology of emotions based on bodily fluids—the four humors—which he described in terms of color: yellow bile, black bile, phlegm, and blood. Once he identified the group to which a person belonged, he believed he could predict that person's responses. This forms the foundation of modern personality theories.

Swiss psychologist Carl Jung carried forward this idea, defining four temperaments by color: cool blue, earth green, sun yellow, and fiery red. Today, chromotherapists practice the principle of healing with color and light to balance energy that is lacking on an emotional, spiritual, or physical level.

Some people say they can see auras—energy fields that surround us—in glorious Technicolor. Most of us don't, but we're certainly drawn to colors that provoke a conscious or subconscious reaction. Who doesn't have a favorite color? Nature has seemingly created a nearly infinite variety of crystalline shades so that everyone will be able to find just *their* color; each green beryl, chunk of yellow citrine, luscious pink watermelon tourmaline, or dramatic black star sapphire will appeal to someone. A stone's saturation, reflection, and vibrancy send subliminal messages that we sense and that elicit an emotional response inside us.

The ancients were entranced by crystal and stone colors, investing them with symbolism. Green feldspar and turquoise were the color of renewal, carnelian and red jasper were likened to lifeblood, and lapis lazuli represented the heavens. Similarly, modern Navajos use turquoise at the center of rituals symbolizing Mother Earth, which provides water and therefore enables plants to flourish. Their eyes are attracted to a color associated with growthand life.

From the beginning, these colors were used in amulets and rituals to make humans feel more contented and protected. The Ebers Papyrus, from 1550 BCE, has the first mention of healing with gemstones, which at that time was done primarily by pulverizing the stone and ingesting it. For instance, "the blood stone of elephantine," most likely hematite, was ground, cooked in olive oil and honey, and eaten. Nowadays, we tend to keep these substances outside the body, if often close to the skin.

> "Why there's not a color on land or sea but is imprisoned
> in one of these heavenly stones! What wonderful jewelry
> could be made with these subtle phrases of color . . .
> such beauties as we moderns have never conceived. . . .
> Let me have these broken lights—these harmonies and
> dissonances of color."
>
> —OSCAR WILDE

It was hard to pin down the colors of crystals into general shades that we all understand. So many glint with assortments of shades that they would be better described by entirely fresh spectrums. The chapters of this book are divided by color; images of certain stones have been included for their color properties, while others are incorporated for their mineral classification. I chose them from my research, trial and error, my personal experiences, and the many in-depth interviews I've conducted with men and women from all walks of life. Those experiences ranged widely, both geographically and culturally. I spent one sunrise sitting next to a fire pit with a Navajo rock hound as we burned sage; he showed me soil-covered rocks he'd gathered for prayers about life's constant movement, to honor the changing seasons and stages of life. Another time, I stood by Jeffrey Post, curator of the National Gem and Mineral Collection at the Smithsonian National Museum of Natural History, as he contemplated whether to add a rough piece of yellow-green spodumene and the largest nugget of American turquoise ever found to the collection.

When you first observe a colored crystal, your heart might thump and your mind become a whirl of excitement, but ultimately it can relax a mind distracted by the modern habit of incessant multitasking—the result of crammed schedules that actually stop us from being fully productive.

The internet has changed our concentration span; we've trained ourselves to think bite-size thoughts, as media and tech platforms compete for what is a finite amount of attention. We become scatterbrained. But by focusing intently on the colored lights inside a crystal, we can effectively coach our distracted minds to think more clearly and complete more involved tasks. Slowly we can think differently and change our habits, our outlooks, and eventually our lives.

The Right Stone for You

It is impossible to overestimate the effect of color when determining the crystal you want and its influence. It may be the most significant factor in choosing a crystal, as gazing into a mineral with a pure and transparent color can produce an almost tranquilizing effect on the mind. On the other hand, you may prefer your color in an opaque variety. I'm not advocating this as a science, but the sensation you experience when you are near a colored crystal that attracts you is unmistakable. Something about the chemical composition of color, combined with the physical structure of the stone, will result in a psychological response you can't define.

Belief in stones has survived millennia because our human desire remains the same as the ancients'; it centers on comfort, community, purpose, and the notion there is something more meaningful than us. Gardeners undertake annual tasks that are backbreaking and (arguably) ultimately frustrating— because nature is insistent upon doing its own thing. But they are driven to persist, because getting their hands dirty in the earth, nurturing flowers and other plants, is good for the soul. In our hectic, city-centric lives, crystals, too, can bring us a sense of the natural world and become lifelong witnesses to our lives that can travel with us, lending some perspective about daily issues, desires, and our place within the bigger landscape.

So how do you choose the right crystal? The choice, when entering into a store crackling with vibrant amethyst, quartz pillars, pink opal, sparkling golden geodes, and dusky meteorites that are older than coal, might seem overwhelming. The simple answer is that you don't; the crystal chooses you.

Even the most down-to-earth crystal specialists and dealers swear to me that stones talk to them. In certain instances, apparently, they shout quite loudly in their eagerness to accompany someone home. At a crystal reading in Los Angeles a few years ago, a small piece of blue frosted anhydrite, commonly known as angelite, hollered out its enthusiasm to travel back to London with me. Something about its energy shone through and caught my eye.

The most effective way to choose a crystal is through its visual impact and your sheer instinct. Hold your hands over a range of colors, gently moving them from left to right, take deep breaths, and concentrate on fine-tuning your senses to appreciate any stimulation you might receive. Keep floating your hand above the crystals in both directions and wait for feedback.

What can you expect? Your heart rate might alter; you could experience a tingling sensation in your fingers or toes. The reaction can be so subtle it's hard to identify when you begin. It could be a sensation like something hot or cool, or maybe a gentle prickling as your hand passes over one of the crystals. If you don't feel anything at first, spend time looking into the colors. One will glint and connect with you, and your eye will be drawn back to it more than any other.

When a stone seems to belong to you, expect an inexplicable liveliness to ensue. This attraction from an aesthetic perspective is the beginning of the connection between you and the crystal. Trust your gut instincts. Often the stone that jumps out will be the one with the right benefits for you. There are millions of neurons in the gut, which has a complex communication system with the part of the brain that is fundamental to our decision-making process and the expression of our emotion. It will be guiding you; listen to it, and block out the head chatter. Even if you've determined beforehand that a blue calcite is the calming stone you need, if there's something you prefer about the labradorite, follow your heart's preference.

Bear in mind that some crystals have a more gentle vibrational energy than others. This doesn't make them less effective, but you could have a slower route to your goal. Also remember that it is not true that the bigger the crystal or the greater number of crystal points within a group, the stronger the power. Good things do come in small crystalline packages.

When you get your stone home, spend some time with it. "Program" it with your intentions as you turn it over in your hands, to create a bond. This shouldn't feel like homework, but you need to see your crystal each day and basically get to know it better. Try sitting with it, maybe while meditating, or just keep it nearby. I haven't learned to meditate, but with the anhydrite crystal I've acquired recently, I've resolved to take the necessary time. I imagine where she's come from, who pulled her out of the earth, and her life before my bedside table.

If you meditate, engage in a crystal reading, or visit a crystal store, someone will almost certainly mention the word *chakra*. The chakras are the seven main energy fields in the body, which spin at specific frequencies and follow each other up the body from the base of the spine to the top of the head like

ABOVE Organic arrangement of green cacti on wood with rock crystal, pyrite, and polished black obsidian

a rainbow. Emotional, physical, and spiritual energy is focused through the chakra points, so while it isn't obligatory, you might be advised to place your stone on one point in particular for maximum effectiveness. Here is a list of the seven chakras' colors and where they are found.

CHAKRAS

1 Red – root
2 Orange – sacral
3 Yellow – solar plexus
4 Green – heart
5 Blue – throat
6 Purple – third eye
7 White – crown

Every choice is just an educated guess, and your choice of crystal is no exception. I deliberately haven't gone into elaborate descriptions of the stone structures that I'm mentioning, as I don't want to persuade your eye to look for a particular type, shape, or crystal mass. Only you can relish the feel of the right stone for you as you pick it up. And remember, the flashiest is not necessarily the best for your purpose. This isn't like searching for a precious stone, which is about size and carat weight; there are no rules or guidelines. It's simply the aesthetics of crystal form, color, and luster that appeals to you combined with the inner X factor of the stone's energy that you identify with.

A stone can't change you, but it can alter your incentives and evaluations and improve the outcomes. Ultimately the choice of crystal is yours to make, and with the right connection, belief, and determination, you will have gained something with power. These drops of color and light can make the load lighter in each phase of our lives, as well as for our children, young relatives, and godchildren, when the complicated dynamics of adulthood take over.

We all come across the same sticky issues of guilt, relationship problems, and feelings of inadequacy that make it harder to advance to the lives we want. The present is a complex time—insecure and constantly changing; none of us knows what will come next. It makes sense to return to the beginning, to revisit the ancient cultural belief in crystal and stones that is fundamental to our human experience, and apply using a new approach to our twenty-first-century lives.

Caring for Your Crystal

When your stone arrives home, it's important to clean it. Crystals travel long distances, and they could have picked up negative energy from someone else before you found it—the exact thing from which you want protection. Run it under a tap for a minute and pat it dry with a soft cloth, or cleanse it with sea salt in spring water (carnelian doesn't like salt), bury it in earth in the garden for a night or two, or leave it outside under a full moon. Moonstones like a dip in warm soapy water, and burning sage is also cleansing if you move the crystal slowly through the smoke. Hard stones such as amethyst and quartz are fine when soaked in water. Porous or brittle stones such as malachite, turquoise, labradorite, and selenite shouldn't be immersed, as they will dull and eventually disintegrate. I'd recommend wiping them with a damp cloth that has been wrung out. Also, malachite and pyrite contain trace metals, so they could rust in water; pyrite glitters better with oxidization. And black tourmaline and lapis lazuli are sensitive, so another idea is to cleanse them by burying them overnight in a bowl of brown rice grains. Toss the rice away in the morning.

Turquoise is supersoft and porous and has adverse reactions to oil, light, cosmetics, and water so take off any rings before washing your hands and clean it in brown rice or with sage.

Give your crystals a regular cleaning with a makeup brush or toothbrush, as dirt can block their light, but I'd never recommend using anything abrasive such as chemicals or cleaning agents. And remember, crystals are organic; like pearls, they don't like perfume, makeup, or hairspray.

Some people leave their crystals on a window ledge, which is fine overnight, but I wouldn't leave them in sunlight. Pink quartz, amethyst, citrine, agate, and carnelian are sensitive to heat and light, pyrite to humidity, and they can lose color if exposed for lengths of time.

If you live in a city, it's a particularly good idea to wipe away any pollution particles that have drifted in through the windows. Once the crystal is cleaned, it's up to you where you keep it. The sensitivity of black tourmaline and selenite might require keeping them away from hands that could inadvertently break them. If there is an accident, don't panic. A damaged or chipped crystal isn't less beautiful or effective; cherish the pieces you have.

Remember, when transporting your crystals, pop them into a velvet pouch or wrap them in tissue, as sharp or hard crystals can scratch and damage each other. If you have quite a few, don't clump them together. They do like to be near one another, but each needs its own space.

CLEAR

rock crystal

Increasing clarity to recover from burnout

COLOR SPECTRUM:
Translucent or clear; trace elements and minerals can create smoky, yellow, rose, and purple shades

FOUND: Brazil, Swiss and French Alps, Brazil, Australia, England, Peru, Madagascar, and North Carolina and Arkansas in the United States

Every civilization, extending back to the earliest humans, has been drawn to rock crystal, or quartz, for its beauty as well as its vitality. From the beginning, it was thought to possess magical powers. Today, rock crystal's reputation for harboring an all-purpose, one-size-fits-all, curative capacity within its glassy structure remains undimmed. If in doubt about anything whatsoever, it's always helpful to have a piece of quartz in the vicinity. The light of rock crystal encourages a resilient approach to life, so it makes a good stone to deal with the dark and bleak feelings of burnout. Described as "the perfect jewel" by the ancient Japanese, it symbolized space, purity, and perseverance—all of which are valuable assets in the midst of exhaustion.

Virtually everyone I spoke to for this book mentioned they owned clear quartz first, before adding other stone staples they now rely on. They have chosen quartz in various forms, such as clear or white hexagonal spikes, crystals, masses, and spears; masses with inclusions; or small tumbled stones, like milky shiny pebbles or transparent spheres.

An Essential Crystal

In spite of laborsaving devices, we're in the grip of a global epidemic of time scarcity. Working parents navigate a home-life balance while trapped in traffic and sorting through hundreds of emails a day. Perfectionists pile the pressure on themselves as they tackle everything at once, hell-bent on multitasking. One of the causes of burnout is overload.

Rock crystal can make you think about your state of excessive busyness and help you realize you need to slow down, stop, and rest. In the age of artificial intelligence, it's important to remember our bodies aren't machines. We can't pull levers to make us more productive, ignoring human qualities of empathy, common sense, and, most important, sleep. This systemic burnout affects not just those midcareer but also millennials working long hours for minimal salaries while feeling underappreciated and burdened with the

OPPOSITE Rock-crystal carved objects and "Meditators" designed by Marina Cowdray displayed on a fossilized table

unfair expectation they should be both pleased with how life is now and unperturbed by the instability of the future we are bequeathing them.

When I look into the core of a rock crystal, my mind is blown away; the contours appear to have dimensions within dimensions and deep reflections that draw me inside, and I'm hardly aware of distractions that drift into the distance. This makes for a rare respite in the midst of hectic modern life. I've never cracked meditation, but I imagine my crystal has the same effect in quietly balancing things for me both intellectually and emotionally. Over the years, I've collected dozens of teardrop-shaped pieces of rock crystal to hang on my Christmas tree. They look beautiful shimmering like icicles on pine-scented needles, but they have the added bonus of radiating positive energy—which we all know can be useful at family gatherings during the holiday season.

Mayas, Aztecs, and Incas all used crystal as a central part of healing rituals to diagnose and treat disease. They also crafted it into "feel-good" jewels and religious ornaments. Cleopatra used crystal to communicate with Marc Antony; her words of love were carved onto six quartz tablets. Throughout human history, examples of rock crystal abound—from six-thousand-year-old lip plugs to a luxurious rock-crystal pommel set into the blade of a dagger entombed with King Tutankhamun more than three thousand years ago to intricately carved Renaissance objets d'art. Today, the vast crystal-specimen "artworks" placed on walls make a contemporary expression of an ancient message, uniting art and nature.

During Rome's imperial period, large quantities of quartz were imported from India. Pliny mentioned a colorless *trulla*, a wine pitcher with a handle, that had been made from a single block of crystal; evidently crystal wine-serving sets made a fashion statement at Roman tables. The high price of the crystal became even more so when skilled engravers carved it into delicate forms, making the result worthy of imperial rank: both Emperor Nero and Lucius Verus treasured crystal goblets. Pliny wrote that he had seen an array of confiscated crystal sets displayed in Nero's private theater. The confiscation may have sparked the practice of smashing a condemned prisoner's cherished crystal possessions in a final act before an imperial death sentence was carried out. That prevented them from falling into the hands of enemies. When Nero's own overthrow was looming, he also smashed his two favorite crystal goblets in, as Pliny wrote, "the last vengeance of someone who wished to punish his whole generation, by making it impossible for anyone else to appreciate these items."

Rock crystal is the common denominator of crystal devotees, collectors, interior designers, feng shui experts, healers, and artists. For example, British fashion photographer Nick Knight tells me he places crystals as decorations around his home, preferring to keep the white walls (designed by modernist architect Sir David Chipperfield) clear of artworks. He emphasizes that they're not there for any energetic value, but he admits they do make him feel better when he looks at them.

Others are less abashed about their crystals' therapeutic aspects. Japanese organizing expert and author Marie Kondo keeps a purifying crystal in her bedroom, to which she shows respect. When you take care of the things you own, she says, you also take care of yourself. Similarly, model Miranda Kerr sleeps with her quartz "wand" next to her on a nightstand to ensure she's constantly receiving its healing qualities.

ABOVE A stone basin created from rock crystal with a matching soup dispenser

"It's a great stone for gathering, directing, and transmitting energy," she insists, "and it can also transform negative energy into positive energy." Kerr uses the stone to release tension from the body; at the same time, she feels the stone's healing energy transferring to her. Actress and designer Kate Hudson also keeps quartz close. She travels with a bundle of crystals in her hand luggage and says she doesn't feel comfortable traveling without them.

Stress is the modern-day response to feeling threatened by life, which is propelling us toward a protective crystal habit as robust as that of the ancients. Lady Gaga is a fan of the work of Serbian performance artist Marina Abramovic, who in her art explores the influence of crystals and stones on the mind and body, creating sculptural chairs grounded in crystal boots at the base, or supporting the head. The transformation of liquid matter into something solid through the action of time, resulting in geometric formations, has influenced the ideas of energy, endurance, and heightened consciousness in Abramovic's work. She pursues things the rational brain can't explain. She believes positive energy radiates from the minimalist "crystal cave" at her home in New York State, which may have inspired the new lobby of Gaga's Los Angeles home. The grapevine says Gaga is having it measured so it can be encircled with crystal.

Sir Elton John sleeps beside a big rock-crystal heart that sits among a cluster of things on his bedside table—as does Martyn Lawrence Bullard, an LA-based interior designer, author, and television personality. Bullard's home is a green and lemon-tree oasis hidden in the Hollywood Hills that was previously owned by the late actor Dennis Hopper, as well as Ike and Tina Turner when they were married. "I had it saged to get rid of bad vibes before we moved in," Bullard explains. He also placed rock crystal and spheres of pyrite on his sitting-room table alongside a 1930s stone-carved Cartier dish, for the spiritual as well as decorative value. "I believe the energy in a room can change with crystal. Those pieces draw me to touch them every day." Bullard notices younger people in particular are decorating homes with the stone, including model and actress Alessandra Ambrosio, who, like others, keeps crystals in her bedroom.

A crystal trait runs though the Kardashian family of reality-TV fame; Bullard sources crystals for sisters Kendall Jenner and Khloé Kardashian. He reports that Kendall is "obsessed" and has them all over the house. Crystals are attached to Buddha heads, and the drawer pulls on Khloe's baby-changing table and wardrobes are all crystal. "It's for the energy, power, and look," Bullard says. "The nursery flows into the family room, and crystals are in there, too." The refractive qualities of rock crystal illuminate Khloe's sitting-room lamps and the caged crystal wall sconces that light her bathroom.

> "From the circumstance of its being hexagonal and hexahedral, it is not easy to penetrate this substance; and the more so, as the pyramidal terminations do not always have the same appearance. The polish on its faces is so exquisite, that no art can possibly equal it."
>
> —PLINY THE ELDER

Power & Perspective

I personally became aware of auras around rock crystal when I was holding a cold stone against my skin and felt a strong sensation like an afterburn. Crystals have power. Lest I be accused of magical thinking, remember that one particular crystal triggered a vast technological and economic revolution: the silicon crystal. The monumental growth of Silicon Valley is rooted in silicon crystals. As larger and larger single crystals of silicon are grown and sliced into wafers, their mushrooming surface area is covered with ever-more-complex integrated circuits. Entire computers and radios are shrinking in size and price.

On a personal level, imagine that your crystal is programmable, like a computer. The idea is to sit quietly holding your crystal and focus on what

1 Rock crystal spears

2 Rock crystal drop

3 Rock crystal chunk

4 Crystal shell

5 Classically shaped crystal bottle

6 Egg-shaped chalcedony

7 Labradorite chunk

8 Slice of natural crystal

you'd like to transfer onto it while visualizing the outcome you'd like. Allow the stone to hold the pattern of your thoughts for a little while, and the "downloaded" projection will reverberate back.

Of course, this is not "abracadabra" magic, capable of bestowing every wish. You still need to work for what you want. The biggest impact crystal has for me is helping me identify what I actually *do* want, because only when you fathom *that* can you begin to work out how to make it real. Sometimes I hold my crystal up to the sun, or place it on a high table at eye level with a candle burning behind it to see into its frozen depths. Then, slowly and silently, I begin to grasp what might make my life better. I've used it for things as simple as a good night's sleep to finding the courage to change my job description so I could focus on the parts that I enjoyed. None of this happened quickly, but determining the ultimate goal made the breakthrough possible. The expression "can't see the forest for the trees" described my situation at the time. It wasn't until I stared into my quartz with intention that I stopped fixating on daily minutiae, which, like overgrown and persistent vines, had been blocking the direction I wanted to take. Even when the subsequent route was twisty and steep in places, I kept picturing the great view from the top that I'd originally glimpsed looking down into the deepest part of my crystal.

BELOW Rock-crystal neckpiece and geometric-shaped bangles created by Pebble London

Designers Mary-Kate and Ashley Olsen of The Row use the power of crystal in a slightly different way. They have been known to give out palm-size quartz crystals to press and clients attending their fashion shows. Of course, they rely on their innate design talent for success but why not "program" the quartz stones with that intention before the models hit the runway? Think of it as a pretty warranty to ensure satisfied customers and promote favorable reviews.

The full-color spectrum exists within the white light of the crystal, which could be one reason for its great power. That ethereal quality would have struck early humans as extraordinary, and it's this refractive property that draws us to it in this age of burnout.

The hardy mountain climbers of ancient Greece named the rainbow-gleaming stones they discovered in caves near Mount Olympus *krustallos*, meaning both "ice" and "rock crystal." It felt cold to the touch and had the appearance of crystalline water. They knew these solid spikes and spears would never melt because the gods had frozen them. The Romans viewed themselves as the heirs to Greek culture and civilization, so it was natural that Pliny the Elder echoed the same thoughts about the stone, which appeared like water to the eye. He concluded that rock crystal was formed by a congelation of water in dark mountain clefts and caverns where the temperature was cold, which created an irreversible freezing of water; its origin in snow-capped mountains appeared to endorse the idea.

> "Crystal is only to be found in places where the winter snow freezes with the greatest intensity; and it is from the certainty that it is a kind of ice, that it has received the name that it bears in Greek. . . . Rainwater and pure snow are absolutely necessary for its formation, and hence it is, that it is unable to endure heat, being solely employed for holding liquids that are taken cold."
>
> —PLINY THE ELDER

In addition to clear crystal goblets, the Romans kept cold crystal balls in the atrium, the main room of the house, on which they could cool their hands during the heat of summer. Pliny also experimented with the stone as an instrument to concentrate the rays of the sun, so that heat was mysteriously produced from something that appeared to be icy. At the time, this must have appeared as a thrilling magic trick, encouraging the widespread belief in the preternatural power of these stones.

On the Mohs hardness scale, where talc is 1 and diamond is 10, rock crystal weighs in at a respectable 7. That strength, combined with its likeness to water, was used to perfection by master jeweler Peter Carl Fabergé in early-twentieth-century Russia in stone-flower studies, more than one hundred of which survive in the British Royal Collection. Pansies, red currants, and delicate lily of the valley are arranged in rock-crystal vases carved to simulate the curved surface of water lying inside.

Although the stone's name defines the limpidity that Pliny and his peers revered, in modern vernacular, *crystal* has become the go-to description for something with transparency. Yet the stone itself is not "crystal clear." Inner fractures contain water or liquid carbon dioxide that look like wisps of fiery smoke and mist; the ancient Japanese called these the breath of the white dragon. In certain cases, the milky effect is like a thin silk covering; those crystals are labeled *quartz en chemise*. The bubbles, streaks, or clouds are not flaws. Rather, they should be viewed as evidence of the stone's metaphysical power, increasing its individuality, character, and attraction. These extraordinary ciphers are evidence from the natural world that can coax even the most grounded of us to believe in crystal's mysterious qualities.

Quartz stones vary in size; some are so minute it would take thousands to make a gram, while other candle-shaped hexagonal crystals can be gigantic, with spears and spikes up to twenty feet long. They were created more than one hundred million years ago, solidifying into regular patterns, much like building blocks stacked on top of one another, growing into mesmerizing geometric shapes.

Esteemed American art collector and dealer Daniel Wolf measures his mineral collection in tons. He has a home in Colorado—a state famed for the clarity and shape of the crystal unearthed there—and over many years, Wolf has built a collection of single and double crystal terminators, each with naturally faceted definite points at each end. "Art has its own narrative, and so do minerals," Wolf says. "Sometimes there might be five or six different chapters of geological history in one piece. I'm building up a crystal collection dictionary of different pockets [of rock] from Colorado. Each one is different, so it's fun to get variations on the theme."

Wolf arranges these pieces of natural art outside his Colorado home. Others, like a pair of four-foot-tall pieces of Tibetan quartz, sit on plinths in the Upper East Side apartment he shares with his wife, artist and architect Maya Lin. Their Frank Lloyd Wright furniture sits alongside giant rock-crystal plates resting on windowsills. "I have a beautiful twenty-foot-long double-terminated smoky quartz from Mont Blanc. Ropes are used in the summer months to bring them down," Wolf tells me.

Wolf searches for stones from retail dealers in New York as well as at the annual Gem and Mineral Show in Tucson, Arizona. He predicts China as the next frontier for minerals from Outer Mongolia. His fascination has, appropriately, many facets: the geology and time involved in the crystals' creation, the manner in which nature organized the chemical structure, the amazing beauty emerging from the chaos of volcanic activity. "God is your partner; you can't really complain," he says. "Nature is the greatest artist. I'm passionate about them because it's a really rewarding thing to collect."

Although Wolf may be addicted to the aesthetics of crystal, he also credits them for keeping his brain active—enjoying what he terms the "inner dialogue" that the quest for a new crystal provides.

But as Fabergé demonstrated, rock crystal can also be worked into other forms. For thousands of years it was ground and polished into spheres: gazing balls to provide visions of approaching events. The mystical "fairy frost" inside crystal globes persuaded early mystics they could envisage the future, leading to the fortune-telling "science" of crystallomancy or scrying.

"Crystal balls are found in the graves of the Iron Age in England and throughout Europe in the Viking Age. It was the belief in the prophetic and talismanic power of 'magical' stones as a medium, which like a magic circle or a dream or vision, broke down the barriers between the physical and spirit worlds," writes Geoffrey Munn in *The Sphere of Magical Thinking: The Enchanting History of Crystal Balls*. Some of these orbs were mounted in copper and silver with large pendant rings, suggesting they were worn on the body at the waist and neck. Those mounted in gold, like the rare example from the fourth or fifth century in New York's Metropolitan Museum of Art, would have been powerful status symbols. Other crystals were brought from the Holy Land following the crusades of the early medieval era, also as spheres for magical thinking.

By 1582, John Dee, mathematician, astrologer, magician, and antiquarian, reported that Elizabethans were using "crystalline receptacles" as panaceas for illnesses in both humans and animals. During this period, it was believed that good spirits entered into crystals in order to communicate with humans, so stones were often used for divination purposes to retrieve and find lost money or treasure. A strong conviction in the power of magical stones developed within every level of society, and ever since, a belief has persisted that a crystal ball can disrupt the blocks between the past and the future, so they remain indispensable to clairvoyants.

One explanation for crystal's hold on human consciousness comes from North African historian Ibn Khaldun, who wrote on the subject in the fourteenth century: "The diviners while in this state do not see what is really to be seen . . . it is another kind of perception, which is born in them and which is realized not by the sight but by the soul."

Clarity & Vision

Awareness of things outside the physical realm can benefit someone struggling in the darkness of burnout. The stone can act as a crystal screen. Focusing on its light and blocking out the continuous white noise that surrounds us slows you down and allows spontaneous thoughts to bubble to the surface. You may be able to catch a glimpse of what you can change, or of something you want to obtain in the future. The way forward could be quietly illuminated, or the answer to a problem made clear.

Is the status that busyness confers propelling you to burnout? Are you trapped by outdated workplace policies, which could be changed? Could you begin a conversation on family management with your partner? The stressors won't let up, but the transparency of crystal can help you figure out how to change what you can and the steps to take operate in a more joyful way.

A deep-rooted belief in the importance of maintaining the wholeness of a crystal endures. Stone expert Barbara Harris, who divides her time between London and Nantucket Island in Massachusetts, uses the term *water jewels* to describe her crystal furniture, jewelry, and objets d'art, because she shapes crystals using only water jets. Knowing that hot solder or tooling would "bruise" a stone, she learned the ancient technique by apprenticing with a master stonecutter in southern China.

At Harris's London showroom I studied a tray of various colored stone rings and picked out a rock crystal "wrap." It fit to perfection; still I returned it to the tray and tried on a few other examples—because green is my favorite color, and I thought malachite would suit me better.

So why hours later did I leave with the rock crystal?

"Stones choose you," Harris confirmed while wrapping the ring for me. "When you tend to need something, at the right time it will turn up." Harris told me the crystal would help me focus energy and inspiration toward my work. The ring turned up after I'd conducted roughly fifteen interviews for this book, spent hours researching in several museums, and read a stack of books—but hadn't written a single word. Happenstance, serendipity, or coincidence; all I know is that I began the first chapter the day after first putting on the ring. My writer's block had shifted. And it might account for the fact that I've begun this series of chapters about color with a stone that has none.

Harris wasn't a big believer in the energy of stones when she began thirty years ago, but she is now, having seen things she would have said were not possible. Some time ago she was hired as a stone specialist to resolve a dispute between a gem-and-mineral gallery in New York and a client who'd bought a large, clear rock crystal as a decorative art object. He claimed it had clouded.

"There was no chip or fault in the stone," Harris tells me. "It was a delicate situation, but I discovered the client was in the process of going through a difficult divorce. I advised moving the crystal, soaking it in water to dispel the negativity, and gradually the cloud totally dispersed."

It was experiences like this one that banished her early skepticism. "I have a disposition for this," she says. "It was what I was always supposed to do. Crystal doesn't necessarily make the journey any quicker, but when you get there, it all makes sense."

I can't predict the future with my crystal orb. Nor can it give me the heads-up about the inevitable ups and downs of life heading my way, but when I look into it, I do find that I can concentrate on a difficulty more clearly. And the ancient trick of mindfulness does have demonstrable evidence-based benefits.

OPPOSITE Improving circulation with icy natural rock-crystal points during a facial

This is the reason that quartz serves people well in their workspace or a room in which they need to think. On my desk in the office I keep a translucent quartz-crystal vase to help inspire ideas. Similarly, Nick Knight recently posted a picture of his desk-side rock crystal on Instagram with the caption "Afternoon thinking and thinking." But it's Brazilian Armenian designer Ara Vartanian who has set the benchmark for the ultimate crystal-aided workstation. He has created a desk using sustainably sourced thousand-year-old wood from Bahia, which stands on one monumental milky-quartz leg made from a single crystal.

Crystal can also help us see through our perceived limitations, which are a component of burnout. Exhaustion can strike following prolonged stress, and living in the era of "yes, I can" as we do, it's a growing problem for high-performing women striving to achieve perfection. It can take people a long time to realize they are in trouble, and given these women's achievement-focused natures, they are the most reluctant to admit to vulnerability. Quartz's clear vigor can work on the warning signs of burnout, such as cognitive and emotional fatigue, because when it feels as if we are free-falling through darkness, this icy spectacle of nature brings much-needed light. It can provide a more lucid vision of the surrounding landscape, and this sharpening of your vision allows you to appraise the different elements in your life. Crystal can guide you to realize when you are stubbornly clinging to things that no longer serve any purpose. It can buoy you with the resilience required to make some changes.

If I were to sum it up, laying the myths and hearsay to one side, I would say rock crystal has remained popular through the eons because during murky times, holding on to its complex combination of depth and light just feels soothing. In other words, it's just so damn optimistic.

ECE SIRIN ———— Writing a New Chapter

Turkish-born, blonde Ece Sirin was a thirty-year-old communications manager for Microsoft who was scaling the corporate ladder when she fell victim to the stress and fatigue that often comes with giving too much of oneself. In 2001, she'd been given the assignment to launch Windows XP in the Turkish and Middle Eastern markets. She began a life on the road, traveling between the Middle East, North Africa, Turkey, Dubai, and Seattle. Her energy and enthusiasm were helping her dreams come true. She even met with Bill Gates and Steve Ballmer to discuss the future of empowering women through technology.

Nevertheless, Sirin says, "it was a patriarchal society. For a woman, it's hard to function in corporate life, where the work life hasn't been designed by females. I found the male-dominated structure difficult, and thought there must be something wrong with me, and I had to become tough and lose my femininity to get ahead and protect my job." She describes herself at the time as a "working machine." But gradually the long hours and constant travel took their toll—she became spiritually and physically worn out.

One day when visiting Istanbul's Grand Bazaar, Sirin picked up a bag of rock crystals and smoky quartz to place around her desk and living room. "I had no clue previously about crystals or astrology, but I wanted to discover my creative energy, and they opened a new chapter in my life."

She started to reevaluate her working life and began researching crystals, stones, mythology, and health therapies. Eventually, she created an online platform for corporate women to share their experiences.

Next, Sirin designed a small gold Artemis symbol to carry with her as a daily reminder to follow her new philosophy of spiritual awakening. Her followers on the platform became interested in the pretty talisman and in the other mythological symbols she made that held sacred meanings. Slowly, they became a global business.

"I still focus on the crystals for protection from other people's energy," Sirin says. "We live in a chaotic world, and many things we receive are positive, but we don't want the negative around us."

YELLOW

citrine

Fostering creativity to overcome indecisiveness

COLOR SPECTRUM:
Citrus shades from pale yellow to orange and a tawny shade of burnished bourbon in a variety of crystal clusters, spears, and faceted gemstones

FOUND: Brazil; Congo, South Africa; Madagascar; Russia; and California, Colorado, and North Carolina in the United States

There's an old adage that it's a woman's prerogative to change her mind. On the other hand, when she does "chop and change," she's described as "plagued" by indecision, suggesting weakness or even a full-blown syndrome. I'm afraid it's true to some degree: dithering can be dangerous when it is immobilizing.

We seem to be surrounded by a fog of indecision in the world right now—in global leadership and economics as well as the seismic shifts in the way we live. Cloudy times breed uncertainty, which gathers over our personal lives, obstructing the way forward. As the pace of change quickens, our ability to make self-assured decisions becomes critical. When we harbor internal divisions and waver between different courses of action, vacillating among our multilayered desires, our ability to make progress suffers. Writer Sylvia Plath succinctly summed up the costs of indecision in *The Bell Jar:*

> I saw myself sitting in the crotch of this fig tree, starving to death, just because I couldn't make up my mind which of the figs I would choose. I wanted each and every one of them, but choosing one meant losing all the rest, and, as I sat there, unable to decide, the figs began to wrinkle and go black, and, one by one, they plopped to the ground at my feet.

Doubt can dominate when we are faced with weighing the benefits and costs of thousands of choices and options, large and small. Some decisions have huge ramifications and need to be slept on; others are as fleeting and inconsequential as deciding between chocolate and strawberry ice cream. All the same, each has to be made. Our choices determine our destiny, so it's little wonder we find making them so hard.

OPPOSITE Golden light floods in through a large citrine stone, green spinach-colored jadeite, and shards of rock crystal

Joy & Discernment

Citrine is perfect for those of us who employ avoidance tactics, delaying a decision, and letting the deliberation drag on. It never goes far away, whatever stage you've reached, as C. S. Lewis noted in *The Silver Chair:*

> Crying is all right in its way while it lasts. But you have to stop sometime sooner or later, and then you still have to decide what to do.

I have a young work colleague who's gone traveling on another gap year rather than make a decision about a relationship. My own usual avoidance strategy is to blame urgent deadlines. They say there are only two sure things in life: death and taxes. I would add a third: decisions. Being paralyzed by indecision can have dire consequences. If you don't make decisions, you guarantee someone else will make them on your behalf. If you want to influence your own chain of events, don't duck decisions.

It's impossible to feel unconfident with a citrine fizzing in your back pocket; gloom and self-doubt simply can't exist around this stone. In part that's due to its bright yellow color, suggesting sunlight and positivity. Although some citrines can range from pale yellow to a darker shade named Madeira for the treacle color of the fortified wine, they, too, are upbeat activists. Citrine galvanizes the right combination of deliberate and instinctive thinking to dissolve doubt and help you base each conclusion on the best information you have at the time. None of us knows exactly what will happen, but life's actions are prompted by these inner decisions. Making a self-assured choice shouldn't become your impasse.

Yellow was an important color in many ancient Egyptian decorative motifs: the scarab, which embodied the sun and creation, and the lotus flower, which opened on the Nile each morning as the sun rose and symbolized renewal.

The Romans, too, esteemed yellow. When Pliny wrote about *flammeum* wedding veils worn by Roman women, he likened their shades to egg yolk. The bride was believed to be vulnerable to the influence of evil spirits on her wedding day; the veil was worn to ward off these malevolent beings.

The color of the veil was reminiscent of a candle flame, and the word *flammeum* evoked comparison to Flaminica Dialis, who in ancient Roman religion was the wife of the high priest of Jupiter, forbidden from divorcing her husband. The yellow was symbolic, perhaps, for lifelong fidelity to one man.

And I fancy that it flaunted the bright hope of a young couple who'd made their choice in life. Yellow always has the effect of buoying the spirit, whether it's manifested in the sun, Wordsworth's fluttering and dancing daffodils, or warm lemons ripening on a tree.

Citrine is sometimes called lemon quartz, and one possible origin of the name is that it's derived from *citrin*, the old French word meaning "lemon colored." Others link it with the medieval Latin *citrinus*, the citron tree.

It is a certainty that if citrine were a flavor, it would zing on the tongue with a sharp refreshing tang and leave an invigorating aftertaste. During the winter months, many of us swallow a dose of vitamin C in the morning to boost the immune system. In a similar way, when faced with a day of challenging decisions, you might "take" a citrine for immunity from inner hesitancy. When your mind is in a dither, holding citrine helps make it up.

Minerals built into the citrine's crystal lattice are responsible for its finely distributed yellow tint. Geologists say the color is caused by "impurities," but that makes the beautiful color sound like a pollutant, rather than a prized natural phenomenon.

The state of Minas Gerais in southeastern Brazil boasts some of the world's largest deposits of gem pegmatites (gem-bearing granite). The Malaga stone was unearthed there, flashing with twenty thousand carats—making it the world's largest faceted citrine.

Citrine's natural pale yellow is so rare that most crystals labeled as such on the market now actually began life as citrine's purple cousin, amethyst, which is found in the same locations. When carefully heated, it turns golden. You and I wouldn't be able to tell the difference between a genuine citrine and a heated amethyst; it takes a highly trained gemologist. True citrines are also sensitive to heat and radiation, so they shouldn't be kept in bright light or excessive warmth.

The Merchant's Stone

According to some biblical scholars, citrine matches the description in the book of Exodus of the tenth gem set into Aaron's breastplate—although according to others, that stone is topaz. Both stones are golden, and their resemblance remains perplexing. When I questioned the Alexa that sits on my kitchen counter about the difference, she answered that citrine is a semiprecious yellow quartz, similar in appearance to topaz. To add to the confusion, some translations refer to the tenth stone as chrysolite, and the ancient Greeks knew *chrysolitus* as the golden stone. That is enough to convince me that the stone in the breastplate was indeed yellow.

So why citrine rather than topaz? Aaron, the brother of Moses, was the founder of the Israelite priesthood, and his shield was called the breastplate of judgment or decision. At a time when humankind was searching for guidance—divine as well as spiritual—citrine would have been just the stone to inspire a set of good decisions to follow.

During the Hellenistic age, the ancient Greeks discovered citrine lining to be hollow, globular rock cavities, which they named geodes, meaning "earthlike." Sparkling yellow concavities must have appeared like the inside of the sun itself.

There are surviving examples of ancient oval rings made with hammered thin ribbons of gold soldered together at the edges, with a grooved ring in the center to hold a citrine cabochon stone. The jewelry pieces we refer to as a set, or parure, started as earrings and necklaces that share the same motif with the intention of being worn together. Whole sets of wreaths worked into the shape of myrtle, ivy, and grape vines, as well as coiled hoop earrings, bracelets, and citrine-stone finger rings were worn as status symbols on festive occasions. When the owner died, these pieces were buried alongside as a source of protection in the afterlife. I like to imagine that as the ancients amassed these golden objects, the sunny citrine would have offered confidence and comfort as they contemplated the lonely, dark journey ahead of them.

Citrine was also used at the beginning of life, often placed around newborns to provide a golden aura of protection. All cultures, including our own, crave the brightest disposition for their children. I heard recently of a group of pregnant mothers who all bought citrines in preparation for their babies' births, hoping to radiate a golden life force of joy from the corner of the nursery.

These children may grow up crystal-aware, like the young daughter of a Californian friend who sometimes slips a citrine into her backpack in the morning before leaving for school. At first, her mother was worried that her child was feeling the need of protection during the day, but ultimately she decided it showed imagination and resourcefulness. It may be something her daughter will be grateful for in later life.

Citrine has been called the merchant's stone. One myth says it brings prosperity and wealth, which could have been inspired by citrine's similarity to gold. Nonetheless, when a young family member launched a new tech platform (in which I'm an investor) for the filmmaking industry, I visited and left a yellow tumbled citrine on his desk as a gift. That was three years ago; Google is now a partner. Citrine encourages sharing one's good fortune with others—just one more of its sunny qualities.

OPPOSITE Smoky colored citrine decorative handles on Barbara Harris's white cabinet housing her smoky quartz jewels

During the 1970s, the mother of New York designer Paige Novick was an early adopter of citrine, crystal beliefs, saging, and other alternative practices. Novick, who at the time felt conflicted by this upbringing, left New York to study in Paris and work at Chanel. Gradually, she changed her mind. "Crystals appealed to me in a high-vibey, energetic way," she explains. "They are powerful and pretty things."

Novick studied and began to use them in a multisensory way, both as jewels and mixing crystals with fragrant essential oils to amplify their properties. She turned the routine of using them into ritual, and the ritual helped her find a way through conflict. She felt drawn back to New York, where she began her business, incorporating her mother's early crystal lessons back into her life.

In her sitting room, she keeps the books that inspire her alongside a glass dish of rose quartz, aventurine, and citrine. "Citrine is my go-to before a presentation or big meeting," she stresses. "I work with the stone, imagining the meeting unfolding the way I'd like it to. I set my intention and envision that I'm reflecting back on the day, and leave that in my mind, which helps with strength and confidence. I ask the citrine for help with decisions," Novick says. She swears it hasn't let her down to date.

I decided to try this myself before a discussion about a new project. I'd been delaying a finance debate, and I was worried that my request might prompt a negative outcome—or that the committee would take my idea and find someone else to execute it less expensively. I was reluctant and so caught up in weighing the possible outcomes that I spun myself into analysis paralysis. I was achieving nothing and getting nowhere.

Yellow calcite is the stone that Victoria Beckham swears increases personal motivation and drive, prompting the first decision, so which stone should I choose—yellow calcite or citrine? I have citrine, so following Novick's lead, I ran a bath over the stone, added a few drops of essential lavender oil, and then rested the stone on my solar plexus as I soaked. Generally speaking, no one gets a pay raise unless they ask for it, and only I knew the length of time, work, and expertise involved to make this project happen. Gradually, the stone helped me mentally tick off my goal-setting boxes one by one. I evaluated what I wanted to happen and slowly I came up with a clear strategy. The next day I felt revitalized, and I knew what to do next. When the meeting came around, I took the citrine with me for quick thinking and confidence.

Holding on to subconscious patterns creates a thick fog we can't see beyond. Negative thinking influences your life and there are consequences to harboring not-good-enough feelings. Decisiveness can shift psychology.

1 Rock-crystal egg

2 Golden citrine necklace

3 Sphere of smoky quartz

4 Free-form pieces of smoky quartz

Cairngorm, or "Scottish topaz," is another member of the quartz family that is similar to citrine. It is found in brownish yellow and smoky shades in the dramatic Cairngorm Mountains of the Highlands of Scotland. The Celtic tribes, who came to the British Isles around 300 BCE, discovered the stone and named it after the mountains in which it was found.

Some of these stones bearing the color of a faint wisp of smoke have been given the modern label of smoky quartz; others, glinting with the color of golden whiskey, passed hands as citrine. Initially they were used as an amulet to protect against plague and evil. In the Scottish glen where I have a home, the local shepherd still feeds animals water doused with yellow cairngorm to protect them from illness and "enchantment" by bad spirits.

By the seventeenth century, citrine was used decoratively in Celtic-knot kilt pins and shoulder brooches, as well as arranged in the hilts of Scottish daggers with straight blades and black bog-oak handles, which were tucked into the socks of Highlanders. These *sgian dubh* remain a part of formal kilted dress today. I like to imagine that during the dark days of the eighteenth-century Highland uprisings, amid the danger of rapidly shifting allegiances, the citrines set into these weapons helped guide Highlanders. When entering the household of a kinsman, they'd leave the dagger by the door. If they believed the occupant was a foe, the *sgian dubh* would be left outside at their peril, so it was safer to have it secreted in their sock—with one swift movement they would be able to defend themselves.

———

In the Shadow of Cairngorm, the Reverend William Forsyth described how a large cairngorm stone was discovered in 1851:

> The descent to Loch Avon may be made from Cairngorm by the Coire Domhain burn or other of the torrent beds. On the Feith Buide there is a narrow gulley, broken by ledges and falls. On the left side, among the shelving rocks, there is a hole or "pot" about six feet deep, in which the late James Grant, Rivoan, found quite a treasure of Cairngorm stones . . . among them was one stone of enormous size, upwards of 50 lbs. in weight, which was afterwards purchased by the Queen for £50.

Queen Victoria's interest in Cairngorm pebbles was sparked by her purchase of Balmoral Castle in 1842, which remains the royal family's summer residence. A watercolor that is part of the Royal Collection depicts Prince Albert wearing Highland evening dress with an enameled kilt pin of seed pearls and rubies surrounding a large, round cairngorm stone from Lochnagar. Citrine symbolized Queen Victoria's sunny days of marriage to Prince Albert and her love for Balmoral and the Highlands, which prompted a fashion moment in London for cairngorm jewelry. Prince Albert's premature death brought an end to cairngorm's heyday, when the court and the Queen (for the remainder of her life) were plunged overnight into inky mourning clothes, accompanied by black jet jewelry.

The first mention of citrine in print comes from a twelve-volume series of books published in 1556 titled *De Re Metallica*, by Georgius Agricola, a German author and scholar of classics, philosophy, and language. These books were the first mining treatise based on research and observation of natural metals and minerals, and it remains relevant today. (The fact that the first person credited with mentioning citrine was a classics scholar makes it seem more likely to me that the stone's name was derived from the Latin *citrinus*.)

It's interesting that many of Agricola's arguments focus on the necessity of positive decision-making related to the health and safety concerns of miners, as well as prevention of the destruction of lands where excavations were carried out. You could say this yellow citrine–aware mining expert was the first industry campaigner with "green" beliefs.

ABOVE Elongated citrine torque by Andrew Grima, with additional sun-colored stone

Agricola wrote his treatise in both German and Latin, which at the time remained the written language primarily used in scholarly and scientific works. In fact, Georgius Agricola is the Latinization of Georg Baur, the author's real name. The books weren't translated into English until 1912, mainly due to difficulty understanding the many Latinate terms the author coined to describe medieval mining processes. It was Herbert Hoover, then a mining engineer and later the thirty-first president of the United States, working with his geologist and classicist wife, Lou, who eventually deciphered the riddles posed by Agricola's language.

Confidence & Optimism

A stone tends to have its moment in fashion at the time its particular qualities are required, and the sunny, uplifting nature of citrine was in demand during the years of social and economic upheaval from the first World War to the end of the second. In wartime, there were widespread restrictions on the use of precious metals, platinum was required by the armaments industry, and the supply of precious gemstones was very irregular. Women on both sides of the Atlantic began to place a great emphasis on stones of unusual color. When citrine surfaced from Brazil, it was instantly popular.

You could argue citrine provided a practical and less expensive solution to fill the gemstone void, but it also played a cheering and sunlit role at a time when confusion reigned and fear fed indecision. At the time, Hollywood stars such as Paulette Goddard and Joan Crawford appeared in fan magazines around the world flaunting, respectively, a 350-carat citrine pendant and large moon-shaped citrine cuffs. The golden stone may have been favored because it was available in suitably weighty sizes to secure actresses' status in the public's eyes as queens of the silver screen; nonetheless, I like to think that citrine could've helped to keep women's spirits buoyant during these challenging years, when good decisions were vital for personal, as well as national, morale. The beams of yellow light would have spread optimism to thousands who may have been unconsciously following the ancients' trust that the stone held the restorative power of the sun.

Indecision holds us back when we're looking for change. Especially in our twenties, we think we have so much time that we can cruise on indecision, throwing choices to the wind and changing course on a whim. But each big decision we take can shape our lives for decades to come. Enabling us to understand that, while perversely not being frightened by it, is the specialty of citrine. Hold it when making a choice or assessment and it will throw light on the situation.

Nothing is perfect and sometimes a "good-enough" decision is better than none at all; it lets you stop the indecision whirling around your cranium, creating self-doubt and leading to the dead end of immobilization. There's a value in committing to a choice, and slowly you'll begin to feel confidence in trusting your inner voice and intuition. Only by making decisions can we start to progress. And knowing you're moving forward does create a feeling of contentment.

VICTORIA FOSTER   Taking the Helm

"I always had a career question mark hanging over my head," says Victoria Foster. Several years ago, in spite of running her own business making mirrored furniture for London-based interior designer Andrew Martin and being happily married, with two small children, she felt an absence in her life. "I constantly had a nagging feeling inside that I was still looking for something," she says. "But I couldn't define it, or make up my mind what it was."

Foster spent years trying to decide if she should carry on in the same mode or throw everything up in the air and take a chance on discovering a new career. "There was a lot of negative energy," recalls Foster. The question turned endlessly on a loop 'round her head until the day she stumbled across a book on crystals, which sparked her interest.

"I embarked on a mission to find a stone," she says. "Not just any crystal—I can't explain it, but the more I read, the greater I knew it had to be a smoky-yellow quartz." But however hard she looked, she couldn't find one that jumped out at her. Then, on a family ski vacation in the Swiss Alps, she saw the perfect yellow-brown quartz in the window of a small village shop. "I dumped my skis, ran in, and bought it," she notes.

The discovery encouraged a decision. Foster visualized a goal and plucked up the courage to voice her desire to change her life to her husband, a fine-wine merchant, Matt. Shortly thereafter, they quit their careers, took their children out of school, and took a trip to the Sleeping Beauty Mine in Arizona to search for crystals with high vibrational energy and what she describes as "soul." Together, they traverse the globe six times a year in search of crystals, while homeschooling the children.

Today, Foster radiates contentment sitting amid dramatic crystal-cluster centerpieces in their light-filled white-painted Portobello Road Venusrox store.

In the store, she encourages others to make an individual connection with a stone as she did. "Some people don't believe in the power like I do," she explains. "They might buy them as a piece of natural beauty, but then they will only be an ornament and won't do their energetic job." The day Foster found her smoky citrine, the autopilot that had been running her life was switched off. She plots her own course now that indecision isn't part of her life any longer.

ORANGE

carnelian

Empowering action to release old hurts

COLOR SPECTRUM:
Pale pink-orange, red, brown, and shades of rust

FOUND: Madagascar, Australia, Uruguay, India, Russia, Brazil, and California in the United States

We tend to trap our emotional patterns and turn them into habits. Leftover brain clutter from a life event or bad experience is a roadblock binding us to particular modes of thinking and obstructing positive perceptions of ourselves. Negative experiences, as unpleasant as they are at the time, needn't keep us rooted to the same spot. The first trick is to stop identifying with the past and reexperiencing old hurts, illnesses, and situations that didn't go well. Carnelian is the stone that can help you in the quest of deleting past problems—and the damaging mind attacks they leave in their wake.

It's refreshing when you release a past experience that no longer represents who you are. Until you banish those hurtful feelings or lurking suspicions, you sabotage the possibility of taking control of your emotions and turning around your relationship, business, or life purpose. Coco Chanel said, "Nature gives you the face you have at twenty. Life shapes the face you have at thirty. But at fifty you get the face you deserve." This is the best reason I know to stop carrying toxic feelings around: we become the emotions we hang on to.

A Tool for Letting Go

The ancient Egyptians likened carnelian to the color of blood, although in my eyes the stone has a russet orange shade. But I share their notion that this stone is a life force to restore vitality and it can definitely make things appear brighter and more manageable. "Red brought nearer humanity by yellow" was how Russian artist Wassily Kandinsky described the color orange. Orange combines physical energy with mental wisdom. It's the color for anyone with low self-esteem, which is often the sticky residue of an emotional blockage. Using this orange stone, you can begin to leave unhelpful things in the past, speak out, and assert yourself.

OPPOSITE Add a dash of orange power into the kitchen with a fiery hand-carved Fabio Salini carnelian bowl

The stone's name originates from the medieval Latin *cornus mas*, the wild cornelian cherry, but is often confused with *carneolus* or *carnem*, denoting flesh. Either way, however, we can imagine a stone like a red cherry burnished with bronze. Carnelian was one of the earliest gemstones used in decorative jewels and ancient beads. Examples of perforated carnelian jewelry dating from the fourth century BCE have been found on the neolithic site of Mehrgarh in Pakistan. In Islam, carnelian is sacred, associated with the holy city of Mecca, the birthplace of the prophet Mohammed, who wore a carnelian seal set in silver as a ring. Gem cutters still engrave small prayers on carnelian to turn away envy and promote luck.

This cherry-orange shade of carnelian reaches deep into your inner core, lending real energy to help you blast through the blocks you've erected for yourself. Carnelian doesn't do passivity—it won't allow wallowing while you nurture a blockage, or sulking as you cling to the status quo in the hopes that things will turn out good in the end. Carnelian likes action and the commitment to leave old feelings in the past. With it, you can reboot an inner gusto for life and the willingness to take a risk.

Carnelian's sunset color comes from natural tints of iron oxides such as hematite, which mixed with water in caverns where the crystal grew to form stripes or bands like light moving swiftly over desert sands. In contrast, the carnelian found along the Narmada River on the west coast of India have a more brownish color. Historically, to add brilliancy, a natural form of heat treatment was used to tweak the orange. The stones were placed into trenches in the sun and left until they baked to a more vibrant shade.

Carnelian offers power and freedom, so it's small wonder the poster boy for this stone was Napoleon Bonaparte. According to nineteenth-century gemologist Charles William King, Napoleon discovered a carnelian seal on an Egyptian battlefield that bore the inscription "The Slave Abraham Relying on the Merciful God." King wrote in his two-volume work, *Antique Gems and Rings*, "The First Consul picked it up with his own hands during the campaign in Egypt and always carried it about him. . . ."

From Egypt, Napoleon's army moved northward into the Ottoman territory of Syria. In spite of initial success, however, his army was forced to withdraw. I fancy the carnelian could have helped enable him to leave this legacy of defeat in the past, increasing his courage on the battlefield, so that he ultimately conquered much of Europe and came to be regarded as a military genius.

OPPOSITE Sunset-orange Armonie Minerali carnelian stone ring by Pomellato

Recently, I was scheduled to deliver a speech to two hundred or so people, including my editor in chief, managing director, and representatives from the Prince of Wales's office at Clarence House. I wanted to be persuasive and garner support for a charitable initiative as well as stress the importance of crafts and skills within my industry, but an event from my past was weighing me down.

Years ago an investigative journalist decided to aggressively interrupt and heckle me in the midst of a radio interview. A lighthearted conversation about fashion trends switched without warning into a political discussion. It left a blockage and fear about saying the wrong thing in public, which with the constant presence of mobile phones has only increased. A wrong word or other faux pas can now easily be captured and endlessly replayed and reposted—an idea that haunts me.

To put this baggage behind me and become fearless in the face of this test, I began working with carnelian, using it to help me reassess the situation and interpret events under a new light to erase the fear.

First, I voiced the fear and wrote down my negative associations about public speaking onto a piece of paper. Then I burned it in a symbolic release. I've also made an "action board"—a Pinterest images collage of successful speeches, enthusiastic audiences, and carnelian stones to activate positive pathways in my brain. Every time I look at the board, I see a powerful message reinforcing the result I want.

I wrote the speech with my carnelian in hand, feeling a rising sense of anticipation. When I stop and examine the feeling, I realize it's not the familiar dread in the pit of my stomach but something new, which—dare I say it?—feels more like excitement. Whether this is a placebo effect or that I've tapped into some energy from the stone doesn't really matter. I feel relieved simply knowing that, even in the face of possible disruption, I can deliver my message with a calm sense of purpose.

I'd been told that carnelian acts on the slow side, and as the stakes of this speech were high, I took no chances. While preparing, I held a stone in each hand, double dosing, to reach the feminine and the masculine regions of my brain. Determined not to rehash the past scenario, I also bathed with the stone. And it came with me in my pocket while I made the speech.

Imagine how persuasive an orator Napoleon must have been to command an army to follow him into war, as well as how forceful he much have been as parliamentary speaker to be able to garner support for his coronation at Notre-Dame Cathedral, becoming the first Frenchman to hold the title of emperor in a thousand years. His passionate style of speaking was used to great effect around the world, as he tossed aside hostile audiences, making crisp declarations of his decisions in the style of the imperial Roman. His ultimate inspiration was Julius Caesar, whose bold speeches and announcements in the Roman Senate were articulated in a fearless, heroic tone.

> "Carnelian is a talisman, It brings good luck to child and man . . . it drives away all evil things; To thee and thine protection brings."
>
> —GOETHE

Glyptic arts (a name taken from the Greek word for "carved,") were widely practiced in Roman times and took two main styles: intaglio, in which the image or design is carved into the stone; and relief, or cameo, in which the background is carved away so that the design stands out from the surrounding background. It's possible that Napoleon's carnelian seal stone may have been a Roman intaglio, a word taken from the Italian *intagliare* meaning "carve." These personal seal stones were used to mark property or "seal" and authenticate documents. Often they were worn around the neck as pendants, or at the waist, with a modest handle for easy use.

The seal stones in rings during this period were almost exclusively carved from carnelian. Measuring 7 on the Mohs scale, the stone is an ideal candidate for chiseling and cutting. Seals were symbols of status, authority, wealth, and virtue. "Some Romans chose simple self-portraits of themselves, whilst others selected attributes of their business, such as the deity associated with their trade or images of the commodity in which they dealt" writes Thomas Holman in *Multum in Parvo: A Collection of Engraved Gems*. These personal seals were often buried with their owners. Surviving examples, as well as depictions on tombs and temple walls, provide an important and detailed view into the lives of the ancients and their belief in crystals and stones. C. W. King wrote this about the origin and use of the carnelian seal stones as interpreters of ancient history:

> To the archaeologist, or the inquirer into the usages of domestic life amongst the ancients, engraved gems are invaluable authorities, supplying as they do the most authentic details of the forms and construction of innumerable articles connected with the uses of war, of navigation, of religious rites, of the games of the circus and the arena, and of the festivals and representations of the stage, with the costume, masks, and all the other accessories of the scenic performance. Let any one, though totally unversed in this department of antique knowledge,

cast his eye over a good collection of impressions from gems, and he will be both surprised and delighted, if a classical scholar, to perceive how much light is thrown upon ancient customs by the pictures which will there faithfully offer themselves to his view.

Carved gemstones have survived in greater numbers from the ancient civilizations than almost any other form of art or sculpture. One hieroglyphic text above a scene inside the tomb of Aba at Deir el-Gebrawi, Egypt, which dates from the age of the pyramids, translates as "lapidaries boring carnelian." Similarly, an ancient papyrus in the British Museum mentions a "purveyor of precious stones."

The rough crystals would have been carried on the backs of men or pack animals to the workshop, before being roughly shaped into beads by a combination of chipping and grinding. Hand-powered wooden drills were used in conjunction with quartz-sand abrasive, and it's thought the beads were ground and polished by rubbing them across a rock slab or rolling them in grooves plowed out of gritty stone blocks. It's not known exactly how these minute beads were created so fine with long perforations, but it's suspected that the hole was drilled first, before the body was rubbed away. Researchers also remain baffled about how the elaborate miniature scenes depicting heroic, theatrical, and mythological stories were carved using basic tools on such a small area without magnification.

Today's gem artists have a wealth of sophisticated equipment to create their crystal fantasies. The *maître d'art* who sculpts bowls, figures, and jewels from carnelian and other stones for Cartier in Paris relies on micromotors, diamond powder, and powerful binoculars to magnify the engraving tool, which is no larger than a pinhead.

During a recent haute couture week in Paris, I noticed crystals creeping into fine jewelry collections, as the fashion houses investigated new ways to craft these precious stones. Piaget used white quartz. Chanel carved Mademoiselle's favorite camellia blossom out of magnificent rose quartz, presented with pearls draped over rock-crystal pyramids. Boucheron's new apartment high above the Place Vendôme glinted with crystal and stone tables and rock-crystal domes over diamond jewels. Vast crystal specimens in the Galerie de Minéralogie et de Géologie formed the backdrop for the new Les Galaxies de Cartier collection of spiky particles of metaquartzite and pyrite, sizzling with the orange patina of fire opals designed to represent the tension between heaven and earth.

Health & Courage

Thousands of years ago, ancient jewelers could hardly have imagined the extravagance of today. They had to settle for stringing orange beads on linen or leather thongs alongside spacer beads of bone or ivory, wood or pottery, glazed faience or glass. These pieces of jewelry were designed to be worn for several reasons: status and display of wealth all played a part, but the fundamental and most compelling purpose for these amulets was to protect the wearer from mysterious and hostile forces. Carnelian's color was symbolic of life-sustaining blood, power, and vitality; thus it was worn as a safeguard against natural phenomena such as flood or drought, as well as disease and accident.

In a time when gods and goddesses were believed to rule over Egypt's sandy wilderness and the natural world held supernatural powers, carnelian was directly connected to the rising sun. The lion was the sun's protector, which is perhaps how the idea of carnelian manifesting courage first began.

Pharaoh Tutankhamun was buried with a small gold bracelet that featured a carved carnelian swallow supporting the sun's disc as well as several pairs of carnelian earrings. The stone was also used decoratively in patterns of block borders inlaid on collars and on the death mask of his casket.

Man has invariably tried to produce materials with which to imitate precious stones, and Egyptians were the forerunners in the art of imitation, producing glass with red, green, and blue colors to imitate gemstones. They described these at the time as "melted stones." Although carnelian pebbles were plentiful and could be picked up in the eastern Nubian Desert without much difficulty, carnelian was nonetheless mimicked using a type of quartz and an orange-colored paste. Minute bubbles of air trapped inside gave the stones a texture that made it difficult to distinguish them from the real stone. According to some experts, the decorative furnishings of the tomb of Tutankhamun demonstrate this; some were cataloged as inlaid with carnelian, when glass would be more accurate.

Yin & Yang

Synthetic and manufactured stones may have their place when used as decoration, as the ancient Egyptians discovered, but in my view, only a natural product preserves within it the extraordinary energy of its creation, capable of arousing in us a wonder and provoking questions about our place on Earth. Crystals and stones have a magical significance pulsating with the power of their fabrication and glory of their visual beauty. These attributes, melded in a symbolic color, are the prerequisites of their beneficial properties.

Artist Kandinsky ascribed more than one quality to the color orange. Writing about the joyous confidence of the color in his 1911 book *Concerning the*

1 Indian agate sphere

2 Rough shards of
carnelian neckpieces

3 Carnelian spheres in both
paler and darker shades

Spiritual in Art, he said, "Orange is like a man, convinced of his own powers." Forgive him; this was written in another age. Orange is also about feminine power. Carnelian won't merely convince a woman to believe in her own strength; it will enable her to enact it.

Carnelian is often referred to as the "survivor" stone, because the more porous host rock on which it's formed disintegrates and erodes away, leaving the hardier carnelian free to be swept away into streams—an appropriate metaphor for the benefits of leaving the past behind if ever there was one.

There are rare references of carnelian classified as male and female based on their color. In "An Essay Towards a Natural History of the Earth," from 1695, John Woodward wrote:

> The common carnelion has its name from its flesh color . . . which is in some of these stones, paler, when it is called the female carnelion; in others deeper, called the male.

This could be the reason that carnelian balances our inner opposite energies of yin and yang: we need both to find an equilibrium.

In *The Curious Lore of Precious Stones*, published in 1938, George Kunz cites the rare *Lapidario del Rey D. Alfonso X*. Written in the thirteenth century, the book recommends the wearing of carnelians "to those who have a weak voice or are timid in speech, for the warm-colored stone will give them courage they lack, so they will speak both boldly and well."

Carnelian gives you the courage to face challenging situations, while releasing you from negative thoughts that hold you back. When a blockage is ignored, it will resurface later in the guise of anger, anxiety, insomnia, or fear. An egg-shaped carnelian with a rounded point makes a handy ally, as the egg symbolizes new beginnings. Sit with it quietly and try to relive a troubling incident as an impartial witness. If you notice uncomfortable physical sensations in your body as the memory awakens, use the egg as an acupressure or reflexology tool on the place where it hurts. Then you can choose how to react differently to this emotional turbulence, as you breathe deeply and release the tension. Visualize it being swept away from you, moving downstream like a carnelian freed from the restraining rock.

You might have to try this technique several times, but on each occasion interpret the incident with less involvement and reaction, with the awareness that you don't want to fall into the same trap again.

Carnelian is said to be good for people who are preparing for a major physical accomplishment such as childbirth or running a marathon. Carnelian, one friend tells me, is her dose of vitamin orange for the spirit; she uses it when she feels sluggish. It gives a sparkle to the eye, and it also works on deeper issues, like feelings of shame or hurt. Another friend keeps it nearby to protect her when an envious family member comes to visit, reminding her that her relative's self-doubt and insecurity need have no effect on her.

Everyone has an upsetting incident or two (or more) lurking in their past. It's so common that I'm surprised that carnelian isn't first on people's lips when they talk about their crystal kits. Emotional blockages can drag you down and disrupt your life by keeping you hitched to something unpleasant. It is far better to carry a carnelian with you than these old offenses; I promise you it's much lighter in weight and spirit. Carnelian can help you override these negative feelings and restore your get-up-and-go and motivation. Make it your personal "cheerleader" and you will begin to think creatively. You can disrupt that haunting message in the back of your mind until you can't hear it any more. In the space you have cleared, you will have planted the seed of spiritual power.

Carnelian will be on your side whether you're battling through a blockage or simply struggling with day-to-day life. The goal is to feel fearless, which can be transformative. When new opportunities arise, carnelian can help mobilize you so you're ready for action. Blockages can be stubborn adversaries, and no one wants to feel they're in permanent combat mode. With carnelian's positive outlook, you can share the burden, and a load will be lifted and shifted behind you, to where it belongs—in the past.

CHARLOTTE GORDON-CUMMING ——— Thriving Despite Trauma

In 2008, Charlotte Gordon-Cumming was working as a musician. Married to Nicholas Evans (author of the bestselling novel *The Horse Whisperer*), with whom she had a young son, the couple had a good life. Then on a trip to Scotland, the couple mistakenly ate a deadly webcap mushroom, which caused total renal failure in both of them. To stay alive while waiting for compatible kidneys for transplant, they had to endure a grueling regimen of dialysis for several hours every other day. "I found the whole process extremely difficult, and many times I wanted to die," Gordon-Cumming recalls.

In the midst of dialysis, she traveled to a health clinic in Monterey, California, to experience alternative treatments, working with a qigong master to try and heal herself. A health practitioner practiced crystal healing on her every day for two or three weeks, placing coppery-colored sandstone, carnelian, and quartz on her body; his hands rested above her kidneys to try and kickstart them out of illness. She felt a palpable power.

"While the crystals were on me, we talked about my earliest memories," she says. Anything that came up had to be dealt with, and I had to forgive myself, as well as the person who may have done wrong to me. I was made aware of transgressions, recognized them for what they were, and let them all go."

Eventually, both Gordon-Cumming and her husband underwent life-saving kidney transplants, but she credits the stones with helping in her recovery: "The crystal healing released a huge cloud in me and helped me enormously through this episode. I was still alive and knew I'd been given a second chance, so in a way the poisoning opened me spiritually. I began to pray again in a profound way, and talk to angels, guides—really anyone to help me."

In the midst of her crystal healing, she'd received strong guidance that she should stop her music career and create a House of Comyn fashion brand of vintage-style floral-print dresses, velvet jackets, and fabrics. When I met her in her London home, I noticed an orange crystal on the table with carnelian and Scottish granite pebbles. I realized the room has a distinct orange glow emanating from ochre-striped patterns on fabrics, rugs, throws on earthy-colored sofas, and decorative objects in sunset shades.

"I'm nature based," Gordon-Cumming explains. "I've always loved stones. They are symbols of purity to me. I have a deep sense of connection with their shapes and colors. They speak to me." She says she places crystals in all colors in the bedrooms of her medieval manor in the English countryside, and a large rock quartz lies on Evans' desk. "He likes the look of them," she says, "but won't buy one for himself. But he says to me, 'Whatever it takes, Char.' I like quiet spaces with crystals around, but I never try to convert anyone."

She has come through the trauma looking strong and healthy. Her tangerine and orange stones have helped resolve the guilt and blame associated with continually reliving the horror of the experience and the emotional post-survival minefield.

"Most people die from the type of mushroom we ate, because they don't get themselves to hospital in time. My story was not to die of poisoning," Gordon-Cumming states confidently. "I didn't want to live in fear of the past, or be the mushroom girl anymore. I realized I was meant to live because I had a mission, a new career, and a lot to do."

PINK

rose quartz

Nurturing love and compassion to increase connectedness

COLOR SPECTRUM:
Pale pink to dark rose, in crystalline masses and hexagonal crystals

FOUND: Madagascar; Brazil; South Africa; India; Canada; and Colorado, Connecticut, and South Dakota in the United States

Life's ride is smoother when our emotional center remains in check, and rose quartz is one of the most nurturing crystals you can find. Emotions aren't meant to be entirely static, but this stone can keep them bobbing away in a gentle rhythm rather than swinging wildly to and fro. Intense emotions can muddy our thinking and skew our reactions and responses to others. I imagine rose quartz serving as a counterweight for feelings, keeping our emotional scale in balance so that we're neither thrown sky-high nor tossed to the earth with a resounding thump.

The Love Stone

"I couldn't even start to tell you how many crystals I have," model, actress, and businesswoman Naomi Campbell recounts, "I keep a black tourmaline and a rose quartz in my bag, always. They signify protection and love, which is nice to have with you when you're traveling around the world every two seconds."

A chunk of rose quartz on your chest can ease the heart of its wounds; its soothing vibrations act as a balm to the emotions, reminding you to keep connected to others and to move forward with love as the focus. I keep my own pink, rocky rose quartz specimen from Madagascar on a table in front of a bay window in my drawing room. It sits high on a stand and reflects into the glass crystal sphere next to it, where it looks like a dusty-pink mountain range. I placed it there to draw love and harmony into the room, which lies in the center of the house; I picture rosy pink vibrations in the air spreading silently from room to room. Visitors often comment on the tranquil atmosphere, which is how I know my rosy massif is doing its stuff.

It never crossed my mind that I would need the benefits of rose quartz when I bought my crystal twenty-five years ago. That was before my blended family came about, before the challenges of being a stepmom, and before the swirling tension of teenage angst became part of the atmosphere.

OPPOSITE Mountainous Madagascar rose quartz placed as the beating heart of the house; a scent bottle carved from pink quartz; Fabio Salini rose quartz dish and pink opal earrings

Fortunately, pale-pink rose quartz is not called the "love stone" for nothing. It is a source of compassion, able to spread understanding in its support of all forms of love: familial, romantic, and unconditional, as well as tenderness for the wider community.

None of us ever gain immunity from familial, business, or friendship relationships turning sour for innumerable reasons, but pink quartz, buzzing with rosiness, keeps you focused on kindheartedness, even when relations hit rock bottom. Rose quartz can work with you on what seem like overwhelming events, and with a tiny pink flicker of hope in the corner of a room, you'll have faith that things can change.

"I use rose quartz for confidence," says India-based designer Marie-Hélène de Taillac. "I had a difficult childhood, and I believe it works. Stones have another purpose than just looking good; they connect you and protect you." She took no chances when she became a mother, dangling crystals above her son's stroller and bed and keeping them around her home in myriad forms: rock-crystal and aquamarine lamps rest on tables with crystal Chinese checkerboards, and a table mobile dances with a mixture of rose quartz, tourmalines, aquamarine, and amethyst.

Beauty & Serenity

A type of early facial mask made of rose quartz has been found in ancient Egyptian tombs. In mythology, Isis, the feminine archetype for creation and goddess of fertility and motherhood, used rose quartz to maintain her youth and beauty.

Another myth passed down the millennia about rose quartz tells of Aphrodite, the goddess of love, beauty, and youth, pricking herself on a thorn in the forest where she has run to save her lover Adonis, who's been wounded by Ares, the god of war, disguised as a wild boar. Aphrodite realizes she's come too late as a drop of her blood mingles with that of Adonis, falls onto a rock crystal, and stains it pink.

Practitioners of Chinese medicine still use rose quartz–tipped acupuncture needles to deepen the curative effect. Similarly, Australian model Miranda Kerr, a new-age goddess with a flawless complexion, rubs oil on her skin with a pink quartz rollerball to soothe it by increasing oxygenation.

My beauty therapist, Caroline Gregson, also instinctively understands the benefits of the stone. She gently rubs a cold rose-quartz nugget over my skin as part of my treatment, and I sense an icy rush of air through my head, blowing away tired and stressed feelings. I leave invigorated as well as with smoother skin.

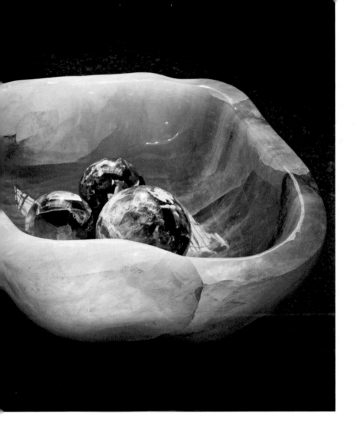

ABOVE Polished rose-quartz bowl with Mexican fluorite spheres

The idea is to take a smooth and polished piece of rose quartz and rub it softly, revolving the stone around fine lines and hugging the curves of the face. It will feel cold as it gets the blood circulating and firms the skin; it's particularly successful over the jawline. The ancient technique of facial massage is more efficient now with modern roller tools, making it easy to do yourself. Courtney Cox was recently seen using a rose quartz roller to stimulate her complexion in a Manhattan restaurant. It kick-starts fibroblasts, and more blood flow brings more nutrients to a sluggish skin. After a while, the stone begins to warm, which I take as a sign it has finished its work.

Tension builds in the muscles of the face as much as in the neck and shoulders, and a rose quartz can feel like a "mini lift"; when we feel lighter, it always shows in the face. Sometimes lapidaries create "puffy" hearts from the stone, like a domed cabochon carved into a three-lobed shape. Using one of these hearts in your regime can act as a reminder of inner love as it vibrates around the skin, giving you an outer glow. A rose-quartz stone is also good for promoting beauty sleep. Tuck one under a pillow or place it on a bedside table to help you relax and fall into a deep rest.

An insanely lavish skin-glow experience would be to bathe in a vast rose-quartz bathtub, like the one I've seen on the island of Murano in Venice. You could imagine Cleopatra having it filled with donkey's milk each morning for her bath; the rose quartz would have helped to smooth her skin, to keep her wits about her, and attract Marc Antony into the bargain.

Not long ago, I spent a day working in a studio on a *Vogue* photo shoot with legendary makeup artist Val Garland, who had model Duckie Thot in a chair. When Garland moved about cleansing Thot's face, I kept hearing a gentle knocking sound. It turned out that Garland always carries a few bags of crystals in her pocket to keep away any negativity while she's working.

She showed me three small linen bags. From the one labeled LOVE, she poured out a collection of tumbled pink quartz, agate, tourmaline, aventurine, and rhodochrosite, which is another pink stone for a compassionate heart.

"When you walk into a room and meet a celebrity for the first time as a makeup artist, you have to go straight up to them and make them feel safe and comfortable in your hands. It's a really big ask," Garland says. She has

to get up close and personal with people, clutching their faces and applying mascara, and she's aware this can feel invasive and too intimate for a first meeting. To help her models feel relaxed, she wears crystal rings and keeps her pockets full of crystals. Another pouch, HEALING, also revolves around rose quartz, but it includes smaller pieces of tourmaline, rock crystal, jasper, and sodalite.

The shoot could have been fraught and stressful because we had to wait until early afternoon to begin, which left minimal time to get the pictures we needed. But with Garland's pink stones in hand, the atmosphere was calm and everyone was relaxed. The result was that we made some great pictures for the magazine.

At home in London Bridge, Garland keeps large pieces of rose quartz; some are loose and others are tied to pipes with copper wire. "It keeps a gentle energy in the house," she explains, "and wealth—because I use it to remind me not to throw money down the drain."

———

These days it seems the complicated machinations of politics are always with us. Sadly, we're all subject to political activity at many levels. It happens to a greater or lesser degree in most offices or businesses, and these can become miniature versions of governmental conflicts as individuals try to acquire power and influence at the expense of others. It's an emotionally exhausting game and ultimately pointless exercise—and one that diminishes self-worth. The disconnection it fosters makes collaboration and teamwork difficult for everyone, as it dilutes the sense of working toward a common goal.

A rose-quartz paperweight on your desk can serve as a pink memo to remind you that you're energetically connected to everyone in the office and to think benevolently about them all. If you don't want to be placed in a competitive situation, there's always another approach. One way is to uncomplainingly get on with the job and let your work do the talking.

———

As children, our subconscious minds are sponges, readily absorbing the patterns of parents, caregivers, and wider family members who, in an ideal world, would manage their emotions in a healthy way. Unfortunately, that is often not the case. We learn by downloading other people's behavior patterns at an age when we have no tools to process negative emotions. These patterns remain embedded, so certain events, or triggers, elicit the same reaction from you as an as adult as they did when you experienced them for the first time as a child.

Although we share DNA with our family members—from susceptibility to illness to eye color—behavior patterns are primarily learned, not genetic.

OPPOSITE Rose-quartz hearts and free-form shapes with a clear box of assorted crystals on the desk of Jess Diner, *British Vogue*'s beauty director

We can control the environmental factors that surround us and work on personality traits to change how we react. We can adapt our environment and activity. Rose quartz provides a gentle way to let go of uncomfortable behavior that doesn't reflect who we've become, helping us take responsibility for the atmosphere we need to flourish. It allows us to step away from the past with love and without a sense of blame or betrayal. We can face stressors when they pop up again, but we'll be better placed to make the type of response that will serve us well in the future.

Vivacity & Openness

Besides the hazy and cloudy rose quartz, colored by inclusions of miscellaneous minerals or other natural elements, there's a type of transparent quartz called "pink quartz" that owes its color to a different process. You're unlikely to encounter this stone as it's exceptionally rare, occurring as clusters of transparent crystals. Originally it was discovered during the late 1930s in Oxford County, Maine; then a larger deposit was unearthed twenty years later in Brazil, which remains the primary source. In 2013, one unique example discovered in Minas Gerais, called "La Madona Rosa" for its glittering deep-pink crystals, sold for $662,500.

The color of pink quartz is attributed to elements of aluminum and phosphorous in the crystal lattice, as well as, in some cases, high-energy radiation in the earth where they grow. Rose quartz contains trace elements of titanium and manganese. However, in the late 1990s an investigation was conducted into rose quartz from a number of different localities around the world, and the results showed tangles of extremely thin pink fibers in the majority of them, so a new school of thought believes these fibers cause the rose hue. Extraordinary natural phenomena produce these pink shades, and whichever stone you choose can have an equally dramatic effect on your heart. It's the soft color of feminine energy that you're looking for to inspire gentleness and kindness.

Rose quartz is too cloudy to make a faceted gem; an almost transparent specimen would also be extremely rare and valuable. No matter its form— natural crystal, tumbled, cabochon-cut—or its depth of color, our interest is in its talents for cherishing and nurturing.

————————

There are accounts of rose-quartz beads dating from 7,000 BCE discovered in Mesopotamia (modern-day Iraq). Early cultures in America also used it as a talismanic amulet; specimens have been unearthed in the Black Hills area of South Dakota, where thousands of pegmatites were formed 1.7 billion years ago.

1 Tumbled rose-pebble neckpiece with rhodochrosite spheres from Arizona

2 Natural pink and red colors embedded in green ruby fuchsite spheres

3 Ruby- and rose-quartz rings

4 Ruby and rose eggs and free-form shapes

Despite that history, pink isn't a color often associated with the ancient world. The strong shades of lapis lazuli, carnelian, and malachite, with their colorful reflections of the natural world, were more appealing to the ancients. Pink is more representative of modern life. Even the word *pink* itself is relatively recent, making its first appearance in the *Oxford English Dictionary* during the seventeenth century, as a word to describe pale red.

What we call *rose quartz* can straddle the pink line from the palest pastel to a vivid, nearly purple shade. To call it candyfloss pink would be deceptive; its color is not the fluffy pink of objectified princesses or the bubblegum hue associated with Barbie dolls. It sits nearer on the spectrum to pink diamonds, which can have a profound effect. In my experience, the effect is far more durable than a temporary sugar high. It can stay with you for the long haul, keeping you energized all day. Early-twentieth-century surrealist fashion designer Elsa Schiaparelli became pink-struck upon viewing the 17.47-carat bright-pink diamond, called the Ram's Head, on the finger of sewing-machine heiress Daisy Fellowes, and wrote the following:

> The color flashed in front of my eyes. Bright, impossible, impudent, becoming, life-giving, like all the lights and the birds and the fish in the world together, a color of China and Peru but not of the West—a shocking color, pure and undiluted.

Schiaparelli thereupon introduced the new term *shocking pink* for bold women. Although generally rose quartz has a subtler and lighter shade than shocking pink, its results can be strong and stunning. Less is more when it comes to this stone, which suggests a vivacity that can embolden. You don't need to scream to be seen or heard. A sherbet roseate can have a strong voice, as the writer George Eliot observed in one of her poems:

> These gems have life in them; their color speaks, say what words fail of.

Environmentalist, columnist, and jeweler Sheherazade Goldsmith, the author of *Slice of Organic Life*, says, "I keep a rose quartz on my bedside table for love, forgiveness, and letting go." When she first acquired the crystal, it encouraged her to literally "let go" of everything on the table that had previously resided there—piles of paper, objects, and an accumulation of things from around the house were cleared away and now dwell outside her bedroom. An entire redecoration of the room took place around the pink quartz. She took all distractions off the walls, emptied drawers, and moved her many precious books to shelves outside the room. Now only three objects remain in the bedroom: the rose-quartz egg, a candle, and one Ganesh ornament. "I like soft things in my home. When I spot the pale pink quartz, it gives a sense of femininity and calm as I get into bed," she says.

Goldsmith bought the crystal in Morocco. She travels frequently and likes the idea of bringing back a piece of the earth as a memento of the places she's visited. "Stones are so complex, beyond anything we understand; there's something so ancient and powerful about their history," she says. Goldsmith believes their energy comes from the force used to make them: "I've got to a point as my life has got busier that I'm looking for a way to achieve peace. As I'm more aware of physical dangers, I'm also looking for protection."

She makes sure that the pink glow is the last thing she spots at night, which always gives her a sense of peace.

In Greek myth, Eros, the god of desire, bestows love in the form of rose quartz. The stone can make a special gift for a young girl at the age she is likely to first experience romantic love. But if a young girl clings to a rose quartz dreaming that it will automatically attract love, she will be disappointed. It doesn't work that way, but it will help her be better placed to recognize love should Cupid's arrow strike—and help mend a wounded heart, should it go wrong. Rose quartz makes a good companion for young people struggling to find their identity; with an open heart, they are more likely to discover the inner values they are meant to rely on and share as they venture into the future.

Parents, too, should keep a rose quartz close by when their children leave the nest and they slip into a type of mourning. This stone is good for the heart and heartbreak in all its forms. During midlife you can feel weighted down by a heavy heart and detached from family members who are moving on with their lives. Wearing a rose quartz close to the skin will remind you that other things are waiting in your future, including more love and life.

My own crystal is too heavy for this use, but if you hold a rose stone to your chest and visualize the pink igniting your heart space, it can be comforting. One friend of mine calls it her "bubble bath for the emotions." If you feel unloved, hold the stone and remind yourself of a phase when you felt positive and strong. Remember that expressing love from a compassionate heart will always transport you to a new way of feeling.

Sometimes jealousy and resentment are directed at us, stemming from a relationship gone sour. There might be nothing you can do about that. Not every relationship should be repaired at all costs, but rose quartz can deliver relief from the ensuing disappointment. And if it can't be mended, rose quartz will reassure you that spreading love remains the best way forward, because that's how trust and hope can reawaken.

Always return to your stone for a quick fix when you feel too emotionally overwhelmed to put your insecurities back into perspective. It will rekindle the joy of sharing. Tension, disappointment, and disconnection invariably crop up throughout our lives from time to time. Sitting with your pink flare will always lighten your heart.

ABOVE Wearing rock-crystal earrings and a rose-quartz-and-pearl pendant
by Harris Zhu to keep the pink energy in focus

JESS DINER ——— Keeping in Touch

A large pink quartz rests on the desk of British *Vogue* beauty director Jess Diner, who's always used crystals at the most important milestones of her life: when she's felt vulnerable, at risk of being disconnected, or simply invested in making a situation work to its maximum.

The first time Diner was "prescribed" rose quartz was when visiting Soneva Fushi resort in the Maldives to write a spa review. Diner had a crystal healing treatment and was advised which crystals she should carry with her; rose quartz was at the top of the list.

"It was a transitional time in my life because I was starting a digital and entrepreneurial area that was new to me, so I thought it was a good idea to reassess what I needed and what would help me," says Diner, who carried a piece in her bra on her first day working at Birchbox, a New York City–based online beauty subscription service.

Since that time, crystals have been her companions at her wedding, the birth of her son, and when she was offered her dream job at British *Vogue*—after which she had to overcome the pangs of guilt stemming from leaving her two-year-old son and the time restrictions the job would place on her home life.

An acrylic box of rose quartz and other crystals helps her safely to the other side of these moments. Inside the box glints more rose quartz, malachite, tourmaline, red tiger's-eye, and jade. "Everything that people thought used to be a bit kooky or a bit niche is now mainstream, because there's a general movement for people to be conscious of their well-being. Having a crystal reading is now the equivalent of someone popping out for a blow or acupuncture," Diner says.

What's propelling this new crystal age? "We're so far into the digital world and discussions about our future with robots, that I think there is a backlash to return to simplicity, ancient ritual, and rediscover the purest form of nature," Diner says. Does it work? "Yes, 100 percent," she replies without hesitation. "It gives me a confidence and stillness that I love and helps with creative flow and ideas."

At her wedding, Diner walked down the aisle with a stone tucked inside her bra. "I don't like being the center of attention, and I was nervous, but it helped me stay calm and connected," she states. She still has the stone at home, carefully stored with other memorabilia of the day. "I didn't wash the crystal, so when I take it out I feel all the emotion of the day again," she says. "I love the different ones that have marked these special moments and times I've needed to draw on a higher power. It's quite cool."

RAINBOW

agate

Learning patience and persistence to reduce restlessness

COLOR SPECTRUM:
White, red, blue, gray, or brown, in masses with banded patterns as well as translucent stones that can appear to hold ancient ferns or fossils trapped inside

FOUND: Brazil; Czech Republic; France; Russia; Uruguay; and California, Idaho, Montana, Oregon, and Washington state in the United States

Although restlessness isn't comparable to an illness, it has become one of the widespread maladies of our time. Restlessness sets in when the life we aspire to—or feel entitled to—remains frustratingly out of reach. As little children, many of us were encouraged to have dreams and desires. Saying what we want to be when we grow up is the first autonomous declaration of intent for our adult life. But often the feeling of contentment that we assume will arrive automatically once we reach maturity eludes us. Instead, a feeling of disquiet inhabits our lives like the fulfillment's changeling. Do more of us experience this now? Possibly, as technology has magically opened new horizons that reveal infinite choices that lie tantalizingly just out of reach. A trove of options is there for the taking, but how do we grasp the right one for us?

Agate will help in this quest. Agate has a lower vibrational frequency than other stones, but that's all to the good. By stabilizing and strengthening inner resolve, it helps banish feelings of restlessness. It simply takes time to work, but its property of mood elevation will support you along the way.

Agate is there for the long haul, and you need time to decide the right direction. You may have had different desires hiding in the shadows for some time; you need to sift through them before pursuing the right one. Remember Aesop's fable about the tortoise and the hare—slow and steady wins the race. Friends of mine are currently wearing his-and-hers agate pendants as part of a couples-counseling technique to restore strength in the marriage, keeping them mindful of each other to banish the restlessness they're feeling in their relationship.

In the ancient world, every color of agate was believed to have its own particular medicinal strength: red agate protected against spiders, green against eye disease, gray fought intestinal problems, and brown repelled poisonous reptiles. For the purposes of this book, I'm banding the colors together to suggest that agate's overall "rainbow" effect can offer respite from restlessness.

OPPOSITE Exotic collection of landscape jasper, Madagascan agates, and red crystal, with a New Guinea necklace arranged beneath a painting from the Cusco Peruvian School

Strength & Direction

Mankind has been relying on agate since the dawn of time. Stone Age spears and arrows have been found with agate tips and other artifacts in gravesites of Neolithic people as well as in early Bronze Age sites dating from 3200 BCE, particularly around Knossos in Crete, where great strides in metalworking and granulated jewels were made. The first mention of agate appears in a treatise titled *On Stones,* written around 300 BCE by a Greek natural scientist named Theophrastus. He referred to agate as a beautiful stone that was highly valued. Both he and Pliny the Elder, writing two hundred years later, agreed that the stone was first discovered along the riverbed of the River Achates (now called Dirillo) in modern southwest Sicily. Pliny's views of the stone's value differed, however. "Agate was a stone formerly held in high esteem; but now held in none," he wrote. By his time, agate was plentiful, having been discovered in numerous locations around Europe.

An extraordinary agate seal stone was discovered relatively recently in a tomb in southwest Greece near the ancient city of Pylos, where a lavish array of grave goods, such as precious stone beads, gold rings, silver cups, intricately worked swords, and ivory combs were buried with noblemen. The carved scene on the stone, measuring just over an inch in length, depicts the war between Troy and Mycenae related in Homer's *Iliad* hundreds of years later.

Agate was an ideal material for hard-stone carving, and skillful gem artists were often commissioned to re-create the heads of distinguished men on the stone. In the same way that a contemporary celebrity might entrust only a favorite photographer with their image, noble Greeks or Romans might have relied on one of a few chosen engravers to depict them. These early stone "selfies" weren't simply about seeking a likeness; the portraits displayed proof of accomplishment and the value and meaning of a life.

Julius Caesar sat for many gem portraits, and these became a trend as others emulated this method of flaunting success—life was short, and the desire to carry the evidence of accomplishments was great. Nowadays, people's likenesses are stored forever on social media, whereas the permanent image or stone resume of the ancients was buried with them. They may well have viewed it as imperative to carry testimony of a life well lived with them into the afterworld. It's not so different. Posterity is whatever we imagine it to be.

Agate is mostly formed in volcanic rock, where trapped gases have escaped through cracks, leaving hollow cavities, pockets, or seams into which seeps liquid rich in quartz molecules. This process repeats, with liquid containing other mineral impurities, such as iron and manganese, forming contrasting bands. The filling pattern continues until the space is full. The colored bands follow the wavy contours of the cavity where the crystal has solidified, producing curved, irregular, and multicolored patterns on the stone. These "cased" holes are hard, so when the softer surrounding lava erodes, they stick out of the rock. Left to their own devices, these nodules eventually release themselves to be tumbled and rolled in rivers and torrents.

Agates were discovered in southwestern Germany's old volcanic fields near Idar-Oberstein, when land was being prepared for planting. A farmer picked up several nodules, which looked like potatoes. It was only when they were broken open that the clouds and zigzag patterns of blue and green dendrites in the agate revealed themselves. A great agate harvest resulted, founding the German stonecutting industry, which still exists in the region today. The stones were cut and polished completely by hand until about 1400, when the technology evolved to harness the nearby Nahe River to provide energy to power lapidary machines.

The oldest agates in the Western Hemisphere, about a billion years old, were formed around Lake Superior in Minnesota. Upheavals of nature over millennia made steam-vacated empty pockets of basalt, which flowed out of the thousand-mile Midcontinent Rift, where agates were formed. When the basalt released the agates, they flowed through the upper Midwest, while others are known to have traveled down the Mississippi River all the way to the Gulf of Mexico.

Unless nature has opened the nodule by breaking the agate against a rock, it needs assistance to reveal its inner world of sparkling banded and striped glory, sizes range from that of a pea to a specimen unearthed in China that weighed sixty-seven *tons*. I have a large slice of agate from Oregon with pale violet and purple patterns spiraling to the center. Some areas are quite translucent while in others I get a sense of depth. I can trace the intricate nature of the patterns inside, similar to circles on a sliced tree trunk revealing its age, which create a wispy mauve-frosted kaleidoscope.

A Certain Magic

The Greeks described a stone that was girded with stripes like a snake—most likely an agate. The surfaces with extraordinary markings must have appeared like something from another world to the ancients. Agate was the stone that encouraged and provoked action, lending the wearer the personification of strength, particularly when worn in a ring.

Pliny the Elder wrote about some of the virtues of agate's patterns and spots:

> The magicians make other distinctions in reference to the stones; those, they tell us, which have spots upon them like the spots on the lion's skin, are efficacious as protection

against scorpions; and in Persia, they say, these stones are used, by way of fumigation, for arresting tempests and hurricanes, and for stopping the course of rivers . . . the stone that is of a uniform color renders athletes invincible.

I don't expect the agate I possess to have such an extraordinary effect; it is about gradual progression rather than overnight success. It does strengthen you to take necessary day-to-day steps in the right direction, which is something only you can know. If that's a daunting thought, it's good to know that in the realm of the agate, nothing is considered to be negative—every experience has a positive lesson. And even on a purely superficial level its beauty offers distraction to a restless spirit.

Pliny described the many varieties of agate: wax, blood, coralline, myrrh, and dendrachates, a Greek word meaning "treelike." The latter is what we call moss agate. A celebrated poem on the virtues of agate, ascribed to the poet Orpheus in Greek myth, stated that anyone wearing a tree agate upon their hand would please the immortal gods.

> "Who comes with summer to this earth,
>
> And owes to June her date of birth,
>
> With ring of agate on her hand
>
> Can health, wealth, and long life command."
>
> —VICTORIAN VERSE

About ten years ago, I bought a pair of moss-agate earrings. The stone has inclusions of chlorite, resulting in green fernlike veins branching through like fanciful trees against the milky background. Moss agate had a fashionable moment during the mid-eighteenth century. It was set into buttons and bracelets; in the prized collection of forty rings owned by King Louis XV's longtime mistress, Madame de Pompadour, several featured moss agate surrounded by diamonds. Madame de Pompadour found her stability and emotional security at the heart of the notoriously conniving French court at Versailles, where her steadfastness and dependability allowed her to change status from mistress to close friend, confidante, and political adviser of the king until her death in 1764.

I imagine that the delicate veins in my flat disc earrings are like the shapes that frost forms in winter on glass windowpanes at Versailles. They come with the bonus of enhancing reflection, persistence, and endurance, which are helpful in the battle against restless feelings. The earrings may swing from golden discs but ultimately they provide a feeling of stability through patience and inner calm.

Other types of agate are also named for their appearance: plume agate boasts feathery designs across the stone; cloud agate shines with a dark center in the midst of a cumulus-white background; straight bands are formed in ribbon agate;fortification agate has a zigzag banding, reminiscent of defensive ditches around ancient forts; and iris agate produces a spectacular rainbow display when its thin bands are lit from the right angle.

Many agates are effective in getting you moving along the right path, so you needn't restrict yourself to a particular variety. When I hold my shadow agate in the sun, the light refracts through the surface of the translucent band before bouncing off the adjoining waxy luster of the opaque stripe. When I move the stone, the light disappears into shadow. Shifted the other way, the light returns, like walking through a forest, one foot after the next.

The circles in banded agates spiral into a black dot that resembles a pupil, which led the Romans to believe the stone was effective against the "evil eye." They imagined an occult force had been preserved within the stone and could influence those in contact around the wearer. Eye agates were sometimes used to form the eyes of idols, as gemologist C. W. King explained:

> It symbolized the third eye now known as the Pineal Body. Clearly the gray tint of the eye of stone approaches in color the matter of the human eye. The importance of this peculiar organ, which lies upon the corpora quadrigemina of the brain in front of the cerebellum, was held in great respect by ancient scholars who regarded it as the organ of occult sight, of inner perception and intuition. This hidden eye is bigger in a child than in an adult, and in the woman it is bigger than in the man. There is little doubt that the ancients regarded these markings on the agate stone as symbolic of the faculties of the high spirit of man, of prosperity in peace, and protection in war.

The perception and intuition that agate promotes make valuable assets for overcoming restlessness; this idea persists in the modern era. Agate is often called the "stone of the wanderer," encouraging the idea that you can make the right change and gain renewed energy to ensure it lasts.

Growth & Protection

Agate was used in ancient cultures to make a spiritual connection to the earth, as well as boost the growth of plants. I came across an interesting myth that farmers should attach agate to agricultural equipment to improve their crops. During medieval times, agates were tied to the horns of oxen to ensure a plentiful harvest.

> "In parts of the Middle East this concept, of its ability to increase rewards from the ground, extends to the powers of agate to revealing where hidden treasure is buried."
>
> —DESMOND MORRIS, *BODY GUARDS*

A Native American man in Tucson, Arizona, told me he'd tested this property of agate by experimenting on cacti. He claimed that pointing an agate at a cactus could make it grow up to five inches taller than one without an agate. Taking his advice, I've planted four agates in the corners of the shady side of my garden, which I describe as woodland because essentially no flowers flourish there. They all point toward a crystal in the center, which faces down toward the earth. I'm going to leave them there until spring, hoping it will have the same effect I've experienced with agates on houseplants. Occasionally, when a potted plant is drooping and fading, I leave it soaking in the kitchen sink with agate pebbles in the water to revive it.

It isn't just the plants I'm hoping to nurture. Fire agates have deep brown, orange, green, and red earthy colors that rise in the stone like a flame. I've planted a few of these in the soil of an indoor shrub to help ground the family.

Vikings and early communities in Saxon England used an ax with a round agate on top to search for treasure. They heated the ax blade until it glowed before pushing the handle into the earth with the agate on the top. Wherever the stone fell and rolled on the ground, they would find their prize. When it stuck to the ax, they'd move on.

Contemporary designers have turned agates into a kind of treasure. Aerin Lauder Zinterhofer, of Estée Lauder, uses the organic shapes of agate geodes as bookends and paperweights with golden rims. At Cartier, carved agate dishes are embellished with art deco-style diamond-and-onyx handles. These lavish ornaments resonate with the ancient tradition of cutting cups, vessels, handles, forks, and boxes from agate—fundamentally anything that held foodstuffs, because the stone was thought to be a charm against the poisons that made a common appearance at Roman tables. Roman historian Suetonius reported that of all the spoils of Alexandria, Augustus kept only a single agate cup.

OPPOSITE Decorative effect of an agate slice on top of a gilded box brightens a dressing table

Noble Romans were intimately acquainted with poison and its effects; toxic plants such as hemlock and aconite, as well as deadly fungi, made a popular choice. They believed drinking from an agate vessel would act as a shield against a poison. The stone was also ground into wine for protection, remaining a prophylactic against poison up until the Renaissance.

The ancients were partially correct, but not for the reasons they thought. Drinking from a stone cup, whether agate or rock crystal, meant you weren't using ceramic cups. Ceramic glaze leached metals such as lead, mercury, and arsenic, giving a small dose of poison with each sip, which over time would prove fatal.

Today, our adversaries or rivals are more likely to poison the atmosphere around us than take us out over dinner, like Nero or one of the Borgias. My neighbor Alex, who practices feng shui, has agate pieces carefully placed in corners to dissolve damaging atmospheres that are draining and cause restlessness; it's best to banish them before they take hold. If you include a protective agate at home in the form of modern stone dishes, try to choose ones with the "eye" as part of the design. Alternatively, there's a plethora available as decorative handles on drawers and boxes, sliced agate cutlery sets, and lamps to place around the house for atmospheric protection.

Agate makes an invaluable ally when you feel depleted by tricky conditions, so use it to restore inner dynamism and get back your motivational mojo. Its mixture of opaque and bright translucent bands represents light and dark, and you can handle both. It's also been credited with the ability to cure insomnia. I can't vouch for that, but then again I don't sleep wearing my earrings.

Agate is often called the stone of eternal youth. I take that to mean that whenever restlessness strikes, it's never too late to find a new way of coping and the stable future you seek. Try holding an agate facing toward the ground and then release any impossible-seeming obstacles to Mother Earth. Sometimes we overthink things, running an endless series of what-ifs through our heads, which can make everything feel worse. We can solve the restlessness with the age-old wisdom of agate, which can help us realize when to resist change and when it's time to discover something new.

Sometimes the pace of technology and popular culture encourages unreasonable expectations about the pace of our personal lives. Real life unfolds slowly, and agate can help you adapt to a more realistic pace. In our busy world it's easy to throw yourself into work and neglect other

parts of your life, resulting in a restless mindset. Feelings of restlessness or mood swings can distract and prove obstacles to growth and progress. Agate can help you identify ways in which you can tailor your lifestyle to be more motivating.

I don't go in for affirmations much, but I like this one for agate: "I am balanced and stable, healthy and whole, and at home on the earth." With agate around, you can move toward the blueprint of your life's purpose, because we all have one. For sure we can fall into a humdrum routine, prompting feelings of boredom or negativity, which can lead to the nagging itch of dissatisfaction. When you've lost your sense of purpose to the daily grind, agate can help reconnect you with your deepest desires.

Listen closely for the messages that might flash into your mind when you use agate so you can decipher them. It may be something you've never tried that's been lurking in your "must-do" list—or a whole new career path. Or you might need to tweak a routine to make more of the parts of your job that fulfill you and make them a regular occurrence.

The rare Ellensburg blue agate, found in Kittitas County, in eastern Washington state, was treasured by the local Native Americans. They believed it linked the throat with the heart, enabling the agate wearer to communicate what their heart knows. In the same way, you can discover the truth about yourself and your hidden purpose, and develop a greater determination and tenacity. Staying in the same place and repeating the same things don't necessarily improve stability. Groundedness comes with feeling more purposeful and ultimately more alive. Agate can help you break free of the restrictions of a restless mind and the density of stuck energy.

BELOW Third-century carnelian from Central Asia designed into a contemporary carnelian tube pendant with diamonds from Glenn Spiro

PAOLA BAY ——————— Finding New Purpose

Milan-born Paola Bay began collecting stone pebbles as a child when she traveled with her parents to the sea in Portofino and when they walked in the mountains of Switzerland. "I was always looking at the ground for the shapes and colors. But it's only in the last three years that I've been seriously into crystals," Bay tells me, going on to explain how she had previously been angry and restless, but that has now disappeared.

Bay's former career was designing beautiful handmade shoes sold at Barneys in New York and around the world, but she grew dissatisfied with the fashion world. The production of a dozen collections a year became stressful and didn't excite her anymore. "I became a slave to it, and the fashion world was changing fast," she says. "I still wear the shoes and get compliments, but it wasn't my calling anymore. I wanted to create something that would last longer than a few months."

When Bay traveled, she brought home crystals. She began meditating and talking to spiritual teachers as she built her large collection of blue lace agate, agates in different shades, watermelon tourmalines, and apatite. She carried some in her pocket and hung others around her neck. Larger specimens were arranged on her windowsill in her living room. "I try to organize them by color—pink, then green and blue, and somehow I make a rainbow," she says.

The first aspect of her life to shift was her negative feelings about family. "I've made peace with my family and my father, who I was fighting with all of my life," Bay explains. "I was born female, and he loves my elder brother. But I can't see the bad anymore and it's better late than never to have an improved relationship with the people around me."

Gradually, Bay realized she still wanted to design, but at a slower pace. She shifted to objects and dinnerware, which might take two years to develop. A few years ago she began working with Howard Schultz on the marketing and communications strategy for expanding Starbucks into Italy. She was drawn by the company's social work and environmental awareness. "They are working hard to resolve the issue of cups. I like working with a group of scientists and designers on environmentally friendly projects and sustainable products," she says.

Since Bay has changed her work life, her restlessness has dissolved. She feels she can make a difference working with a big corporation that has the power to change habits through its innovations. "I'm fulfilled working with young designers and helping them bring their ideas to fruition to save the planet," she emphasizes.

PURPLE

amethyst

Gaining calm and lucidity
to resist dependency

Amethyst soothes overactive minds, and nothing makes the mind more overactive than love. Saint Valentine allegedly wore a pale-lilac amethyst ring engraved with a small figure of Cupid, sparking the connotations of love and courage, every bit as much as rose quartz. In conducting my research, I found the two worked in tandem—most women who owned one also had the other. "I don't stay single for long. I carry a lot of rose quartz, which attracts the male," says singer-songwriter Katy Perry. "Maybe I need to calm it down with amethyst."

Suggestions of love around amethyst continued from ancient times into the nineteenth century. The great love of Victorian poets Elizabeth Barrett and Robert Browning was sealed with an amethyst stone ring engraved with the initials E. B. B. Out of curiosity I looked up Barrett's date of birth: March 6, 1806. The zodiacal gemstone for Pisces is the amethyst, so that fact, too, could have influenced their choice.

> "From passion and from care kept free
>
> Shall Pisces children ever be
>
> Who wear so all the world may see . . . the amethyst."
> —VICTORIAN VERSE

An Antidote to Overindulgence

We can develop an overreliance on anything. Smartphones seem to have been designed to addict us, but we also become dependent on exercise, work, food, relationships, or personal performance. Some people seek to perform at their best 24/7, building an irresistible physical or psychological need. Any behavior that yields an instant feel-good hit of dopamine can lock us into a miserable groove of repetition, and in the end we feel controlled by the dependence.

Amethyst breaks these patterns, because the stone is an antidote to overindulgence. It can help uncover the root cause of an imbalance as well as support the process of overcoming dependence by unplugging from unhealthy attachments. Keeping it close by acts as a mauve memorandum of your newfound intention to treat body and mind with respect.

———————

Amethyst's name is derived from *amethystos*, from the prefix *a,* meaning "not," and *methyein*, "to become drunk." The Greeks believed this purple stone could combat intoxication and foster a state of sobriety. Perhaps this early association of amethyst and alcohol began with Pliny the Elder's thoughts on the stone's color:

> The peculiar tint of their brilliancy, which, after closely approaching the color of wine, passes off into a violet without being fully pronounced.

In his sixteenth-century poem "L'Améthyste, ou les Amours de Bacchus, et d'Améthyste," French poet Rémy Belleau wrote about the myth of Bacchus, the god of wine and grapes, and a young maiden called Améthyste who refused the god's affections. Her prayers to remain chaste were overheard by the goddess Diana, who transformed her into a stone. Humbled by Améthyste's desire to remain chaste, Bacchus poured wine over the stone as an offering, which dyed the crystal a purple shade. He swore from that day on that anyone wearing the stone would be protected from his drunken ways.

Although the ancients used wine to alleviate pain and disinfect wounds, as well as for its intoxicating properties, they recognized a surfeit of the purple liquid drove the drinkers to irrational deeds and chronic abusers to insanity. In this light, Bacchus (or as the Greeks called him, Dionysus) was considered a god with a double nature. He could be kind and helpful, but also cruel and destructive. He embodied in turn a playful, aimless joy and an aggressive, murderous lust for destruction. Drinking out of "sober" amethyst goblets to neutralize the wine was the answer followed by some ancients.

Amethyst's link with wine certainly survived until at least 1750, when Camillus Leonardus, a physician to the Borgias, listed amethyst as a means to prevent inebriation. In 1992, a stash of Renaissance jewels, dubbed the Cheapside Hoard, was discovered in London next to St. Paul's Cathedral. The jewels are thought to have been buried by a goldsmith, who intended to retrieve them later but never returned. Enameled gold pendants feature amethysts carved into clusters of grapes, alluding to the stone's ancient association with wine.

ABOVE Glass terrarium
housing an amethyst geode,
curated by designer Eugenie
Niarchos in her studio

"Drowning our sorrows" is the phrase we use when Bacchus has got the better of us, but amethyst can be a purple prompt to keep the craving in check, to stop us from "drowning" in it and to refrain from "flooding" others with an emotional torrent. "Addiction is a tricky subject when approached honestly: it's basically *Groundhog Day* without the jokes," observed film critic Tom Shone. Given that Netflix is packed with dramas and documentaries detailing modern drug cartels and dependence on prescription medications, it appears we need "sober" amethyst as much as the ancients did.

Amethyst is known as the elevator, because it can lift spirits and help you think more clearly. When emotions begin to feel overactive, it will provide a sense of calm, so they have less chance of bursting forth.

Michael Skipwith, a member of the British General Osteopathic Council and himself an osteopath, is drawn to working with amethyst in certain cases where there's been a major onslaught on a person's body and psyche. "Certainly for people who've gone through drug abuse, which has left them fragmented, amethyst can help give them a sense of boundaries and containment when connectedness has been shattered," he says. Skipwith finds amethyst a calming influence on the nervous system. He places it over the patient's heart during treatment as a point of reference to reconnect them and help them feel more grounded. It makes a useful additional tool when he's working to clear trauma patterns in victims of abuse or torture and people who've returned from war zones such as Iraq and Africa. "I've seen amazing results clearing trauma patterns," he testifies. "They give additional help as people start to piece their lives together again, because crystals give something to hold on to, which helps with feelings of structure and containment."

Power & Tranquility

My own most potent experience with amethyst began one day ten years ago when I randomly clicked onto a real estate website. My first sight there of a house for sale sparked what I can only describe as a potent physical reaction. A shot of electricity fizzed through my body—I knew I would live in that house. The owner wanted a quick sale, so we were pitched in with other bidders in a hurried process. In spite of the stressful process, I was convinced it would work out, because this was the place where I was meant to live.

Two weeks after moving in, I stepped out into the garden and my eye caught a large geode poking up out of the earth. When I lifted it, I discovered a miniature cavern of amethyst chevrons sparkling inside the dark exterior. This was proof for a jewelry editor, if any were needed, that this was meant to be my home. Possibly, the previous owner had positioned the amethyst by the door to place a shield of lilac light around anyone entering or exiting. Or perhaps she'd buried it to cleanse the stone and forgot about it, and so it was abandoned. Whatever the reason for the stone's placement, I feel it called me to my house. It now sits on a mantelpiece, where I see it every day.

> "Amethyst is an ideal stone for enhancement of one's physical environment."
>
> —ROBERT SIMMONS, *THE BOOK OF STONES*

I like to accelerate the calming influence of amethyst by combining it with aromatic plants, flowers, and wood. I have a pair of amethyst earrings with tiny hidden wells that hold drops of essential oils. This design unites the quieting nature of amethyst with therapeutic herbs such as clary sage, lavender, and patchouli.

It was the calming influence of amethyst that appealed to Suze Yalof Schwartz, a former editor at American *Vogue* and *Glamour*, who initially turned to the stone as a way to make bedtime easier for her young sons. "I had three very active and fun boys ages three to nine years," she explains at her Los Angeles drop-in studio, Unplug Meditation. "I didn't want to change that, but did want them to go to sleep at night."

Schwartz placed three large amethyst caves in her sons' rooms, which did the quieting trick and transported them peacefully into their teenage years. When one son wasn't happy at school, she acquired a monster carnelian and arranged rose quartz in all the bedrooms. "Who doesn't want love and luck and success?" she asks. I do believe in crystals and my home has the best vibes. When I touch my crystals, I feel so happy."

When Schwartz opened her Westside studio, one of the classes just wasn't working, so she asked the teacher if there was another type of lesson she could try that would be more popular. They advertised a crystal class, and forty women turned up the following morning. The studio now has five teachers using crystals in meditation classes. She also opened a "crystal candy bar"; clients can take home a crystal to use with Schwartz's Unplugged Meditation app. "People leave the classes feeling great," she says. "I'm not crystal crazy, but I do believe in their energy, and amethyst can make a difference. That's why it's one of my favorites."

Occasionally, Schwartz misses the inspirational characters she worked with in the world of fashion, such as journalist André Leon Talley, but she was determined to create the sort of meditation center she'd like to frequent. The classes aren't long and drawn out, but they quickly and effectively help you

1 Collection of purple and green stalacites from Uruguay

2 Amethyst crystal clusters

3 Spears and plinths of amethysts

4 A necklace of "druzy" amethysts, a configuration of many tiny sparkling crystals on the surface of a crystalline body

gain maximum strength and feel good. She compares this to being around crystals: "If you're intentional about anything, it's helpful to make it work."

Her tip? "Never read what crystals mean first when you're buying one, because you invariably choose what you need."

———————

Amethyst appeared in ancient Egypt as early as the First Dynasty and continued to be used as late as the reign of Tutankhamun. The crystals were weathered or ground into ovoid and spheroid shapes, most commonly worked into beads but also sometimes made into pendants and scarabs.

In Roman times, the color purple had great significance. A violet dye produced from the glands of a certain snail was an expensive, luxurious color reserved for imperial use; a sumptuous stripe of purple adorned senatorial and other patrician togas. Pliny the Elder noted the authority of purple:

> This is the purple for which the Roman fasces and axes clear a way. It is the badge of noble youth; it distinguishes the senator from the knight; it is called in to appease the gods. It brightens every garment and shares with gold the glory of triumph. For these reasons we must pardon the mad desire for purple.

The Romans' obsession with the color led them to dig quarries in harsh environments thousands of feet above sea level among the remote "smoking mountains" of the eastern Egyptian desert. Philip Hewat-Jaboor, chairman of the art fair Masterpiece London, has visited the quarries, now a World Heritage site called Mons Porphyrites, and reports that it remains littered with rough-hewn purple stone blocks of imperial porphyry and partially carved busts of emperors.

From its remote origin, imperial porphyry was shipped to the capitals of the empire, where its purple color attested to divine power and conferred legitimacy on Roman and Byzantine emperors. Emperor Constantine VII lined a chamber in purple porphyry within the great palace of Constantinople, overlooking the Bosporus Strait, where the empress gave birth. The phrase "born in the purple" was used to reference the power of monarchs, denoting the child's future prominence.

Fluorite, another extravagant stone in the purple family transported from the deserts of Iran, was used for smaller objects during the Roman era. It is a softer stone than amethyst and has shifting combinations of purple and green tones that shimmer in dim light. Fluorite's softness made it easy to carve intricate scenes of classical mythology or traditional pastimes.

OPPOSITE Sparkling mauve amethyst gemstone jewelry by Pippa Small

One goblet was carved with emblems associated with Bacchus. Grapevines tumbled down the side of the cup, appearing green until wine was poured, when they turned to red.

Amethysts were also carved. In medieval times, goldsmiths often engraved eagles and lions, symbolizing strength and nobility, onto amethysts, and the stone was used in royal crowns, scepters, and the rings of bishops. A large, faceted amethyst monde sits atop the 530-carat Great Star of Africa diamond on the royal scepter in the British Crown Jewels. The Duchess of Windsor, for whom Edward VIII gave up the British throne, employed amethysts to symbolize the royal status denied her: she commissioned a fantastic bib necklace of twenty-seven large step-cut amethysts, with a large heart-shaped purple stone at the center.

Catherine the Great presided over the Russian Age of Enlightenment and oversaw the establishment of the first state-financed institute for the higher education of women. A fan of amethyst, she sent exploration teams into the Ural Mountains to search for the stone, and she often wore it in the form of girandole earrings, aigrettes, and dress ornaments stitched onto garments. Those stones discovered in Russia have set the benchmark for amethysts ever since; a rich shade of purple is invariably described as Siberian, regardless of its true origin. To simulate stronger shades, the Victorians were known to enhance the pale amethysts with bright foil backings.

The depth of the color purple in an amethyst is determined by trace elements. A "drenched" color would present in glorious regal purple, whereas pale violet stones are called rose de France. Amethysts are sensitive to radiation, including ultraviolet, so they should not be left in sunlight; it can make the color diminish. Amethyst is a pleochroic stone, meaning that light transmits through it in two visible wavelengths, so it appears to take on different shades from different angles.

Stones from different localities have different colorations. Amethysts from eastern Mexico are pale, with crystals "phantomed" so that clear quartz appears on the interior and purple on the outside. Those unearthed in southwestern Mexico are the other way around. The Empress of Uruguay is one of the largest specimens of an amethyst geode ever found. The 120-million-year-old stone stands almost eleven feet tall and is large enough that a visitor to its current home, the Crystal Caves Museum in Australia, would fit inside the geode.

Bravery & Nobility

As we get older, the reasons not to make a big life change multiply. But sometimes a fresh start when ditching an unhealthy dependency is exactly what we need, and an amethyst can help. Smaller stones will work fine, as will any color you fancy from pale rose to papal purple. A small stone placed under your pillow at night may help you to assimilate new ideas and dream well—although there are those who find the effect too strong; it keeps them awake with thoughts and plans.

Historically, men wore amethyst for bravery; Egyptians soldiers carried amethysts into battle to retain their courage. Women, too, have used it when seeking their power. In the 1900s in London, Emmeline Pethick-Lawrence, the treasurer of the Women's Social and Political Union steered by political activist Emmeline Pankhurst, chose purple as an emblem for the group of fearless women pursuing women's suffrage. She announced, "Purple . . . is the royal color . . . it stands for royal blood that flows in the veins of every suffragette, the instinct of freedom and dignity."

A large amount of suffragette jewelry featuring amethyst was produced between then and the outbreak of the First World War. Sometimes it took the shape of a purple heart set with a small green garnet, signifying hope, and tiny white pearls for purity. London jeweler Mappin & Webb dedicated a page of their 1908 catalog to "Suffragette Jewelry," featuring brooches and pendants in enamel, emerald, pearl, and amethyst. Women wore these jewels to preserve their courage during protests, acting as precious badges of solidarity with the cause of women's suffrage, as well as a means to identify other supporters of the movement. Sylvia Pankhurst designed a portcullis, overlaid with a convict symbol and hanging purple, green, and white colors, for the "Holloway Brooch," which she presented to certain suffragettes on their release from Holloway Prison.

It's entirely appropriate the amethyst was their choice. The stone, with its inherent red and blue lights, marries the masculine and the feminine—which was fundamentally the mission statement of the suffragettes. Why couldn't women vote, like men? The desire for purple at this time was no longer about a fashion; it signified nobility of purpose used as a proud emblem when openly voicing a cause, even when it put the women in peril. We modern women have them to thank for bringing us nearer the goal of equality.

In some cases, working with the energy of a home is as important as working on ourselves. Outside factors such as electromagnetic energy or the land on which a house was built can affect the energy inside a building. Bestselling novelist Santa Montefiore's life changed for the better when she was advised by an energy healer to place amethyst caves in her London home.

Montefiore and her family had moved into the house twelve years before, but they never lingered on the ground floor, which felt cold and unfriendly. She recalls, "I'd just started a new book called *Sea of Lost Love*, but it didn't have its usual spark. I sent it to my agent, and she told me I'd lost my mojo. I just felt awful in my office where I had to sit and write all day. I've written a book a year for twenty years and I never have writer's block." Montefiore also began to suffer from tinnitus.

Her office led onto a sunken courtyard where apparently a stagnant pea soup of bad energy lingered. The energy healer staked out the area and specific points where she thought Montefiore should place amethyst caves. "Twenty-four hours later," she says, "I turned on the lights in the room, and the change was dazzling. It felt warm and cozy, my tinnitus had gone, and I felt full of energy and enthusiasm." She was able to successfully rewrite the book.

The Montefiores can now use their whole house. It is liberally dotted with crystals perched in bookcases, on kitchen counters, and in the garden. A clear quartz crystal occupies the desk of her husband, historian Simon Sebag Montefiore, and she keeps another nearby as she works. "I have a rush of energy and feel much sharper if I have rock crystal with me and can tune in more clearly. I know crystals make a difference, amethyst especially, because I've felt it," she says.

It is interesting to see how many of the spiritual properties attributed to amethyst in past centuries are similar to those for which it's used today. Leonardo da Vinci wrote that amethyst was able to dissipate evil thoughts and quicken intelligence. Ancient Greeks used amethyst to calm fears and keep cool-headed in the midst of confusion.

The stone can stimulate the mind into a serene reflection and understanding of your life's experiences and your dynamics within them—and then help you use that understanding and honesty to lessen the hold a toxic dependency has on your psyche. Amethyst is associated with bringing peace to a situation or connection, and that relationship may well be with yourself. Any type of dependency can be a way of running from your internal environment. But we can regulate the choices we make and how we choose to respond to what life brings to our doorstep.

ABOVE Amethyst caves at London's Bamford Haybarn

Amethyst is used to soothe an overactive mind. When you feel peaceful, your breathing slows and your cortisol levels diminish, which can activate a restorative response. That response makes it easier to counterbalance the mindset that propels you back, time and again, to addictive patterns.

Use amethyst to develop a sense of your own connectedness and an appreciation of the root cause of the habit. A boundary of amethyst pebbles can give a sense of self-containment and dispel illusions with which you might justify the old habits. A purple amethyst cave in your home can be the beginning of the end for those irksome issues. Amethyst may be the crystal to help you make the tiny tweak or the big change you need to focus on the things that bring you joy and make you feel good.

ABOVE Carry crystals with you in the form of a quartz drop earring or large
natural amethyst ring by Pebble London

CLAUDIA NAVONE ——————— Choosing Independence

Claudia Navone had been living in Sydney for ten years, working as the fashion editor of *Harper's Bazaar* Australia, when she realized a disturbing fact about her life. Her glamorous life in a fabulous apartment overlooking the ocean and her well-known connections had gained her celebrity status in Australia, and when she announced that she was engaged to be married, legendary designer Alber Elbaz sent her a wedding dress.

"I had a taste of fame. Now I feel sorry for anyone who is famous," she tells me. "The newspapers criticized every aspect of my life, from how I dressed to how many sugars I put in my tea. I lived exactly as I wanted. I was a spoiled and successful fashionista, but inside, so much was unresolved. I needed to change. But I was fighting against my awakening because I was very attached to all the material things in my life."

Suddenly her long-term relationship collapsed. Both her engagement and heart were broken when her fiancé announced he was leaving her to marry someone else. "He thought we were mismatched," she recalls, "and quite frankly he was right. He was very Australian and wanted his wife at home cooking, and I was never that. But I kept falling for the same maverick characters—attractive men, but obviously they weren't right for me."

She had begun to buy crystals before things came apart, unconsciously choosing amethyst, clear quartz, and rose quartz, and instinctively laying them on her heart. In retrospect, she thinks the stones were preparing her for an awakening. Navone gave away most of her clothes—except for the wedding dress—and left Australia carrying two suitcases. She returned to her hometown of Florence to heal.

Amethyst helped Navone detach from her reliance on unhealthy relationships, as it worked on her consciousness, enabling her to understand more about herself. "There had been a lot of genetic abandonment and loss in my family," she says, "but now I have amazing relationships."

Other people began to notice something different about her, something lighter and happier, and she began helping others who were dependent on the cyclical nature of repeating patterns in their various forms. Navone has worked hard and is adamant that everyone needs to empower him- or herself, penning a book of her experiences titled *The Shapeshifter: A Tale from Glitter to Light*. She believes crystals have the capacity to transmit love and light. Using stones helped her feel brighter and learn to live in a better way.

RED

garnet

Improving grounding and stability to minimize anxiety

Stress is an epidemic, and often there is little we can do about our stressors. However, we needn't add to the list by allowing rampant anxiety to control what we do. It is natural to avoid what scares us, but small fears with seemingly little impact can become increasingly debilitating as avoidance starts to limit our lives. Many of us bump up our levels of stress hormones when we fixate on a panic list of incidents that, in reality, pose little or no danger to us.

When we spend time worrying about a problem that might never happen, we are not warding off danger, we are feeding irrational fears. The fundamental problem is not the hypothetical event or incident but, as President Franklin D. Roosevelt famously said, fear itself. Fear can bore in and insidiously undermine our feelings of well-being.

Garnet counters worry by allowing you to take pleasure in the world around you right now. When you keep in mind the positive things that you're grateful for, it will help you stop dwelling on anxieties. As Andy Warhol said, it's important to try to improve things, even when they look bleak:

> I'm starting to think that crystals don't work. Because look what's happened lately when they're supposed to be protecting me—my rug has cancer from the moths, I stepped on a beautiful old plastic ring and crushed it, and I was assaulted at the book signing. But I've got to believe in something, so I'll continue with the crystals. Because things could always be worse.

An Aid to Overcoming

Red is associated with power, and wearing the color in clothing or jewelry can make you feel more motivated and energized. Pliny the Elder recorded that cochineal dye was reserved for Roman generals, and in the Catholic Church, scarlet is the color reserved for cardinals.

OPPOSITE Nineteenth-century floral garnet earrings, an Ann Dexter Jones garnet-and-ruby lariat, and antique red-shaded glass

The idea of garnet's conferring strength probably comes from its uncompromising deep blood-red color with flashes of black. Jacqueline Kennedy Onassis, who surely had a legacy of fearful memories to endure, was pictured wearing a nineteenth-century garnet-and-diamond flower in later life. During the Victorian era, widows were drawn to garnet jewels as a sign of their loyalty and fidelity, trusting that the stone would help them through the time of loss and adversity. Garnet's smoldering red glow helps in dark times. According to the Talmud, a garnet provided the only light on Noah's Ark.

> "By her who is the month [of January] born,
>
> no gems save garnets should be worn;
>
> they will ensure her constancy,
>
> true friendship, and fidelity."
>
> —VICTORIAN VERSE

When our minds drift toward imagined fears, we distance ourselves from reality and waste valuable energy. Fears can be managed by challenging yourself to do what frightens you. Living through the experience and coming out the other side builds resilience, as you realize the fear might not be as bad as you think. Garnet can be an aid in this. Its passionate red color dispels melancholy and settles the feeling of uneasiness, creating the firm grounding of a safe space around you.

Anxiety is often the product of perfectionism; some of us stop doing certain things because our personal standards are too high. Try to think more rationally about what seems threatening when you hold a garnet, and let go of things over which you have no control. Use garnet as a reminder not to hold back from doing anything out of fear of failure.

Garnets crystallize into hard symmetrical cube shapes. They often herald a diamond source nearby. When diamond miners discovered garnets near Kimberley in South Africa, they named them Cape rubies.

The family of garnet contains several varieties. The pyrope garnet takes its name from the Greek word *pyropos,* meaning "fiery." It glows with a lighter shade than the deep red-purple almandine variety. During the 1960s, another slightly different green shade was added to the group. It is called tsavorite, after the Tsavo area of southeast Kenya where it was discovered. Pliny the Elder summed it up when he wrote, "Nothing is harder than the attempt to distinguish the varieties of this stone."

Even the origins of the name *garnet* are perplexing. Some say it's derived from the Latin word *granatus*, meaning "grainlike." But the American Gem Society refers to *gernet*, a Middle English word meaning "dark red." Another theory is that it comes from the Latin *granatum*, for "seed," as the bright spherical red grains of garnet in rocks look something like pomegranate seeds.

Pliny knew it as *carbunculus*, Latin for "little coal," which is why it can ignite a passion for life. For this he may have been following the Greeks. Theophrastus, the father of mineralogy, wrote this description: "blood-red, but like a live coal when held against the sun." In antiquity, gemstone brilliance relied on the external light sources of the sun or fire under which they appeared charged with a magical power. Shipwrecks were a common hazard and the belief was that an infant who wore a red "carbuncle" stone from birth would be saved from drowning.

When you hold your garnet to the sun, it will kindle up the bright red fire inside, which is uplifting. Red has always been the signature shade, and a lifelong obsession, for designer, artist, and businesswoman Paloma Picasso. (Paloma embraced fire engine–red lipstick long before it became fashionable, even producing her own shade of Paloma's Red to wear.) As the daughter of two painters—Pablo Picasso, the twentieth century's most prolific figure in art, and Françoise Gilot—color has been essential to her life. "Color is about light," she explains. "Both we and the world around us come alive with light."

In a series of rings she named Paloma's Studio, she includes energetic crystals such as amethyst, citrine, and green tourmalines. She favors the robust pinky red of a rubellite, which is closer to fiery red garnet and ruby on the color spectrum. Paloma didn't know rubellite existed until 1979, when she joined Tiffany & Co. "For something with that color to exist that's come out of the earth is fascinating. I always think that when you wear a ring, a dialogue springs up between you and the stone," she says. Paloma is drawn to rubellite more than any other stone because she believes its elevating and uplifting color can't fail to make you happy.

Paloma's personal choice each day about what colored stone to wear is ruled by emotion. "When I lived in New York, people often talked to me a lot about the healing effect of stones—like amethyst is good if you have a hangover," she says with a laugh. "People believe in the strength of its effect, but mostly I do that for myself, making my own perception of the color, rather than what they are meant to do."

Her father began a tradition with her when she was young, beachcombing along the Côte d'Azur in the South of France looking for interesting pebbles and tumbled pieces of glass in green, blue, and brown colors, a custom that

she preserves to this day. She brings back what she describes as "little presents" from trips: "On holiday I'll swim to shore from a sailboat and collect pebbles, which I have to carry in my swimsuit. I weigh much more on the way back."

An obsidian bowl she designed contains stones picked up in the Aeolian Islands; others might be placed in the garden of her Lausanne home. "In a sense, I give them back. But now," she says sighing, "I find more plastic washed up from the sea than glass."

Connection & Security

In modern-day Greece, people still believe in the "evil eye." Votive objects are offered in fulfillment of a vow, and icons are often laden with stones and jewelry in exchange for healing. Maria Lemos, a Greek-born, Oxford-educated, fashion showroom director, trusts the ancient Greek tradition of stones that she learned from older people's experiences on the island of Patmos. "When we need help," she says, "we want to hold on to something physical to help us through the difficulties. It's how we make ourselves stronger." Lemos believes the emotions we impart to a stone link us to a joyful memory or a past incident, and they can pull us away from thinking negatively and spoiling potential happiness with gloom. Lemos inherited an aunt's jewel, which has three garnets on the reverse side; to her, the stones signify her three children. "When I wear it, that's my good luck, and it definitely changes the energy you give out, and that you receive back. Positive energy just heals and helps me enjoy exactly where I am," she says.

Garnet is the state gem of New York. The bedrock into which the foundations of Manhattan are driven contains a large amount of garnet. One stone the size of a bowling ball, weighing more than nine pounds, was found in 1885 near Macy's flagship Herald Square store. It became known as the "subway garnet," although it was actually found during a sewer excavation.

At the age of fifteen, Mary Queen of Scots wore a red "carbuncle" at her marriage to the Dauphin of France. The red stone was carved *en cabochon* into an oval with a high dome at the top and flat bottom; it was said to be worth the then-fortune of five hundred crowns. An eyewitness description of the marriage at Notre-Dame Cathedral is recorded at the National Trust of Scotland:

> Mary was dressed in a robe as white as lilies. Her immensely long train was borne by two young girls. She glittered like a goddess with diamonds around her neck, and on her head a golden crown garnished with pearls and rubies and one huge carbuncle.

Imagine the apprehension and fears, both real and imagined, of a young girl, already queen of Scotland and preparing to marry the future king of France. And for some time, the carbuncle lent her security. In 1561, when she became a young widow, she reluctantly left France, where she had been raised and which she called "her dearest homeland," for Scotland, where she met with political and romantic disaster. History doesn't relate what happened to the carbuncle.

———————

In the ancient world, garnet beads were used in conjunction with carnelians. Bead makers and metal workers worked side by side, threading red berrylike stones with golden spacers onto collars and bracelets. A rounded cabochon stone was used to emphasize the eye of an animal or bird of prey, and garnets were often depicted in statues of the goddess Isis, representing her blood and power.

In Later Hellenistic styles, the stones were set in the center of twisted gold bands, decorated with rosettes and reef knots for necklaces and diadems. By the Roman age, there was less emphasis on goldwork and more on the placing of the stones for their own sake.

In China, mandarins wore stones of different colors to signify their rank; red ruby and garnets were the highest level, connoting luck and revitalization. Many Buddhists believe in the holiness of the men creating the amulets, usually monks, and the blessing of the amulet by a holy man was thought to transmit the power of the object to the wearer.

The use of amulets is widespread in Buddhism, as protection from malevolent spirits responsible for illness and other misfortunes. These could be something as simple as a blessed tiger's tooth, fragment of Buddhist scriptures, or a stone image. At its most decorative, during the third century BCE, there are examples of ornate golden-cylinder amulet cases with garnets behind oval openings along the eight sides of the box. A leaf shape at one end is designed to be opened so one can slip in woodblock-printed charms on paper, grains, pebbles, or pieces of silk. Sometimes these charms were fashioned like miniature shrines featuring painted plaques of Buddhist images. Both men and women would have worn these either around their neck, on a cord over a shoulder, or on the topknot or pigtail of their hair.

Strength & Vitality

When she's preparing to audition for a new role, my actress friend sometimes swaps the citrine she carries in her bra for a garnet; the garnet quells her fear while allowing her to demonstrate her passion. "No, it doesn't dig into me," she promises." I just feel a gentle warmth charging up my body."

I prefer to keep my own garnet tucked into the side pocket of my handbag, where it is easy to access in quiet moments. It's easier to focus on the color of the stone when there are no other distractions around. Take time with your garnet to acknowledge small wins each day to bolster your confidence and help you remember not to take flights of fearful fancy.

Garnet is the "warriors" stone; soldiers and crusaders wore garnets on belt buckles, sword hilts, and shields as a talisman against death and injury, as well as to bring peace and tranquility in victory. When you might find yourself in a combative situation, garnet is good to carry against elusive opponents of irrational fear, unpleasant spin, and malicious gossip or lies— which all fare badly in its aura.

Around the turn of the sixteenth century, deposits of small garnets, referred to as Bohemian garnets, were found near Prague. The ruler of the region at the time, Rudolf II, emperor of the Holy Roman Empire, had an interest in astronomy, chemistry, and astrology. He was an avid collector of art and objets d'art, and became the most famous mineral and gem collector of his era. The emperor employed agents to travel throughout Europe collecting works of art and naturalia, including hummingbirds, crabs, shells, and fossils.

One important stone Rudolf owned was La Bella Hyacinth, a large red almandine garnet weighing more than 2,800 carats. When Rudolf moved the court from Vienna to Hradschin Castle in Prague, the collections were housed in a *Kuntskammer* of thirty-seven cabinets containing natural gemstones, uncut crystals, and gem minerals. Rudolf encouraged gem cutters, goldsmiths, artists, astronomers, and scholars from all over the world to move to Prague, and it remains an important center of garnet cutting to this day.

Rudolf suffered from bouts of depression and displayed a fearful and reclusive nature. The court physician, Anselm de Boodt, who had studied medicine at Heidelberg, curated the emperor's collection, suggesting that Rudolf believed in the health benefits of his crystals. De Boodt made many mineral field trips into Germany, Silesia, and Bohemia collecting specimens. Finally, with Rudolf's vast collection at his disposal, he wrote one of the most important mineralogical works of the seventeenth century, titled *Gemmarum et Lapidum Historia*. In it, he makes an early mention of crystal healing and the practice called sympathetic magic, in which, for example, a stone could be used to cure a complaint of a matching color. The red garnet was used to cure heart palpitations and blood disorders. As blood is the life-force of the body, garnet was perceived as a lifesaver. George Kunz wrote about the practice in *The Curious Lore of Precious Stones*, quoting from de Boodt:

> That gems or stones, when applied to the body, exert an action upon it, is so well proven by the experience of many persons, that any one who doubts this must be called over-bold. We have proof of this power in the carnelian, the hematite, and the jasper, all of which when applied, check hemorrhage. . . . However, it is very necessary to observe that many virtues not possessed by gems are falsely ascribed to them.

1 Natural ruby necklaces

2 Tumbled garnet necklaces with agate borders

3 Rough garnet and ruby necklaces

Today we don't use garnet to cure heart tremors; rather we want it to get the heart pumping with courage and power to overcome what we think is a hopeless situation. Bracing ourselves for something bad doesn't make it less likely to happen. Sometimes I have an anxiety and fearfulness that positive things can't last; when anything goes well, I immediately worry. How crazy is it not to enjoy the moment? We can't curate the future to an impossible standard. We need to apply our brain space to something proactive and not expect perfectionism.

When such feelings arise, I hold my garnet aloft, changing my state of mind as I watch the color shift from dark burgundy-wine red to deep purple and the burning coal that Pliny described. Even a small spark can become a warm ember and ignite into a stronger flame. Whatever happens next, we can all cope better than we imagine when we face our fears head on.

There's an energy-sapping exhaustion involved in the panic that anxiety can produce, not to mention the time-wasting fatigue of avoidance. The longer you skirt the issue, the worse it becomes.

Irrational fear is unpredictable; it can come seemingly out of nowhere. Garnet is a gem of faith, so hold steady to the conviction that it will help overcome your qualms—then you'll feel prepared to counter anxiety when it strikes. You will feel an increasing sense of security and trust that you'll be right, exactly where you are right now. Stay focused on the garnet and you can get past the problem and enjoy living with grace, not fear.

| **ABOVE** Natural-faceted garnet bracelet

SHALINI VADHERA —————— Starting Again

Raven-haired Shalini Vadhera was plagued with irrational self-doubt after an investor stole her beauty business. Always a passionate entrepreneur, Vadhera began her first business at age nineteen in India, then became a celebrity makeup artist on *The Tonight Show with Jay Leno* before using her know-how to build the beauty company. But the bad experience with her investor left her disillusioned and nervous. "It was a real challenge to believe in myself," she says, "but I knew unless I overcame it I wouldn't be able to start again."

A friend suggested she consult an Indian astrologer who was visiting Los Angeles. She explained to him the hard time she was having and how her trust in the wrong person had rebounded so badly for her. He advised her to use a red stone to begin to change her energy.

She then attended a spiritual retreat in Sedona, Arizona, famous for its energy vortexes. Vadhera learned about the friendships that weren't good for her and how to be protective of her energy. "I didn't want this monkey on my back anymore, which was fear," she recalled. "I had to clear any emotional trauma from my previous business partner and anything that was holding me back from my future."

The lessons from Sedona and her red garnet helped her realize that she could shift her energy away from anxiety and use it for anything she wanted. At home in Los Angeles, she lay rose quartz in the bedroom to shelter her marriage, and placed garnet and selenite in the core of the house along with celestite, citrine, and amethyst.

Vadhera picked up her career as beauty expert by writing the best-selling *Passport to Beauty*. Her self-esteem improved as the garnet erased her fears, and she began confidently sharing her passion, determined to mentor young women in business to help them avoid the pitfall she'd experienced. Through her Power Beauty Living platform, she organizes workshops and panels to empower young women to reach their highest potential. That venture led an invitation to speak at the United Nations.

The Indian government has honored her with the Jewel of India, the highest award bestowed on a nonresident Indian, in recognition of her motivational charitable work providing solutions for young Indian women in lifestyle, careers, and business.

"I use garnet for protection when I go into a boardroom meeting now," she relates, smiling, "especially with men. I have it by my skin as a shield of protection to give me a warrior mentality. I'm no longer fearful that anyone can penetrate me to get what they want."

BLUE

turquoise & lapis

Finding equilibrium to ease travel

COLOR SPECTRUM:
Turquoise—powdery blue to green, with bright shades of blue stone in opaque masses

Lapis—Deep, dark blue, sometimes speckled with white calcite or gold pyrite inclusions

FOUND: Turquoise—Iran; Afghanistan, Chile; China; Australia; Mexico; and Arizona, New Mexico, Nevada, Colorado, and California in the United States

Lapis—Afghanistan, Australia, Chile, Russia, China, and California and Colorado in the United States

"I'm crazy about crystals," actress Kate Hudson tells me. "I vary them each day depending on what I'm using them for, but since I'm traveling at the moment, I have turquoise with me for safe journeys and protection. I do a lot of intuitive work, and I use blue celestite for that." Today's Stone Age women are global citizens who are constantly on the move, which can cause a kind of travel anxiety. We fret about leaving loved ones behind, worst-case scenarios, and security concerns as we traverse borders, and the resulting adrenaline boost rockets us into a fight-or-flight mindset.

Remember that anxiety is contagious; it wants to travel with you from person to person, so practice calming yourself to reestablish equilibrium before it becomes overwhelming, especially in the confined space of a subway train or aircraft.

When I take off on a flight and look around, I invariably see someone touching a talisman at their throat to relieve stress and help them feel more serene in that moment. Actions, like anxiety, are contagious, so a sense of enlightened composure will extend to those around you, helping all of you to arrive with a clearer mind and in better shape.

Turquoise—The Traveler's Stone

Known as the traveler's stone, turquoise represents the wisdom that comes from all life's experiences, so even cruising at thirty-five thousand feet, it can help you feel grounded and connected to the earth. Often emotions have a defined physical response. If your heart beats faster and your hands or brow get clammy when you fly, the anxiety that causes the reaction is likely propelled by your mode of thinking. Turquoise can help you let go of the stress and make your thoughts more rational, which helps shut down the flight-or-fight response. So close your eyes and take a deep breath while connecting with your touchstone turquoise to offer reassurance that you

OPPOSITE Bright blue corner arrangement of turquoise, chrysoprase, and chrysocolla

can survive the journey. While traveling, it's important to remember that turquoise is relatively fragile and can easily fade or crack. It needs to be kept apart from scent and hairspray.

———————

Medieval Turks believed in the protective power of turquoise, so they tied it onto horses' manes and tack to protect both rider and animal on journeys.

> "Whoever owns the true turquoise set in gold will not injure any of his limbs when he falls, whether he be riding or walking, so long as he has the stone with him."
>
> —VOLMAR, *DAS STEINBUCH*

Other cultures also attach important beliefs to turquoise. On the mantel in my office, I have a small piece given to me by a friend who'd been traveling in Santa Fe, New Mexico. It represents the six Corn Maidens, who, a story says, long ago saved the Zuni people from famine during a time of severe drought. Native Americans believe that the earth is alive and that all things, no matter how small or apparently inanimate, are precious. At one time, as many different words for turquoise existed as there were languages spoken. Turquoise represents inner spirit and life.

Turquoise was already being mined by the Pueblo people a thousand years ago in Mount Chalchihuitl near Cerrillos, New Mexico, centuries before the arrival of Europeans. They built fires against the rock to crack it before working the turquoise out with picks made of antler. The Pueblos used sky-blue turquoise, with its connotation of Mother Earth, as an offering to the gods. It symbolized the truth of the soul and reverence of nature and its cycles. Every shaman kept sacred turquoise for healing; without it, he would have no recognition of power.

For the Zuni people, turquoise bridged heaven and earth: bright blue stones were Mother Earth and crystal was Thunder Father sky. Turquoise was also thought to be sensitive to weather patterns, so the stone was thrown into riverbeds during droughts, accompanied by prayers to the rain god. It was a staple artifact to bring good fortune. Warriors and hunters fixed turquoise to their bows to help arrows speed straight to the mark.

Native Americans' belief in the sacred nature of turquoise is evident in objects unearthed from burials, such as death masks and ornaments. In one grave, nine thousand beads and pendants carved into the forms of rabbits, insects, and birds were scattered around a single skeleton—most likely they had been strung into anklets or necklaces. A turquoise basket found alongside had a design using more than a thousand turquoise stones.

During the seventeenth century, Spanish friar Marcos de Niza traveled to New Mexico. In 1639, he noted the Native Americans' personal adornments, household goods, and even human skulls solidly and skillfully encrusted with turquoise and obsidian:

> The people have emeralds and other jewels, although they esteem none so much as the turquoises, wherewith they adorn the wall of the porches of their houses and apparel and vessels, and they use them instead of money throughout the country.

Truth & Communication

When Native Americans noticed a crack in a stone, they would say, "The stone took it," meaning that the stone had absorbed a blow that they would otherwise have received. You can use that idea as mental preparation when traveling by transferring your anxiety onto the stone. The Zuni people believed turquoise would protect them from demons; for us in the modern age, constant travel is accompanied by its own demons.

The color blue can lend you deeper insight, intuition, and mental peace—good qualities to draw on in the midst of a bout of travel anxiety. Sometimes work or family situations mean you have no choice over a relocation or journey that might force you away from everything familiar. When you find yourself overnight in an alien situation, needing to learn new cultural etiquette and avoiding any symbols of offense, let turquoise be your guide, and know that you can make a stable new life while keeping your identity.

It takes a special stone to lure a woman who flies around the world from Mozambique to Jaipur viewing the world's most beautiful gems. Thirty-five years ago, the light shone onto a lilac-blue sapphire and captivated Lucia Silvestri, design director of Bulgari. "It was a special moment, and I fell in love with this stone," she says. "I didn't want to mount it because I like to look at it, especially when I'm flying. I feel better when I look at it because I have a special relationship with the gem. It's my tradition."

Home is her comfort zone, so Silvestri likes to take the stone with her when she travels. It's the combination of the color and her personal ritual that is important to her and puts her in the right frame of mind on arrival.

She often combines turquoise with malachite or amethyst, but she needs to touch them to feel their energy when she first encounters them, because no two stones are alike. "It's a matter of personality; if the stone has it, then it can immediately talk to me," she says. "And my reaction is to say *buongiorno*. I know it sounds crazy, but I talk to stones."

| ABOVE Cool blue tones in designer Alexandra Jefford's studio

ABOVE Alexandra Jefford's lapis lazuli and malachite art inspired jewelry

Everything has energy, but if and how we perceive varies. Many women I talk to say, "It spoke to me" about their crystal—in which case the obvious next step is to answer it. Even crystal energy skeptics such as Alan Hart, chairman of Britain's Gemmological Association, can have an emotional soft spot for a particular stone. Having completed a research project at Harvard on black opal, which flashes with blue and green lights, one specimen became Hart's "pocket stone" of choice. "Each mineral tells a story of human endeavor as well as natural history, plus an emotional personal story," he says. "When guys pull a stone out of the ground, they remember the feeling they had and it becomes important to them. If you match an emotion and a story to a stone, which is based on a previous incidence, then you always have that in your mind's eye." In this way, touching your turquoise talisman each time can lift your mood, reconnect you instantly to a successful journey, and bring you back to a nice place.

There's a school of thought that turquoise can stimulate the throat chakra to help you communicate, tapping into what Native Americans describe as your "deepest wisdom." Wearing the stone empowers even the most shy to share an understanding, because when speaking truthfully from our inner core, we each have something important to contribute. When mental functions and communication skills are lifted, we will generally be more expressive.

Travel anxiety can affect the quality of your voice, as stress causes muscles in the body to tighten, including those in the throat, neck, and jaw, so concentrate on turquoise as a protector of your vocal performance. The tone of your voice establishes the type of relationship that you want to have with someone, whether it is one of friendliness and acceptance, or not, so turquoise can be used to preserve friendships and make friends out of acquaintances.

Traveling can be turbulent—favorite places, homes, and even countries seemingly ebb and flow around us, each only a temporary perch. The cost of a peripatetic lifestyle can be your sense of belonging and the security of your mental space. The touchstone of a piece of blue primeval rock gives the comfort of ritual and a link to something lasting. Being in transit is like being in limbo, but with rock-solid blue, you always know where you are, even in unfamiliar territory. The experience of travel is a physical act—it doesn't have to come with an anxious state of mind.

Ancient Native American chiefs, Aztec kings, and Egyptian pharaohs all wore turquoise, but it was unusual for women at that time to do so, as female life was linked to hearth and home. Now women can reclaim turquoise, because our travel schedules would bewilder even the bravest warrior. Turquoise gently encourages the wearer to pursue answers and knowledge, and definitely the more intelligence you have about your trip or travel plans, the better prepared and less daunted you'll be. A good tip is to keep it in the car, maybe attached to your key chain, so you never leave the house without it.

> "I've used many different stones in my work and I've always been interested in the stories that surround them and their different symbolic meanings, as well as the lengths humans have gone to get the more precious ones. For my *Treasures* show, I added turquoise to my sculpture of the Egyptian goddess Hathor, as she was the protector of the turquoise miners. Ancient peoples built stories and belief systems around stones. Turquoise is so beautiful and it just comes out of the earth—you'd have to make sense of that somehow and of course you'd think it was divine."
>
> —DAMIEN HIRST, BRITISH CONTEMPORARY ARTIST

BELOW Lapis lazuli in free-form pieces, rings, and a necklace

Some turquoise has a solid, pure color, while "spider web" turquoise has small veins of black manganese or brown limonite. Color varies from blue to green to yellow-green. The green variety is formed as the product of a long-term chemical reaction by acidic groundwater, usually in arid regions, which seeps into rocks containing copper and aluminium.

The name *turquoise* comes from the stone's journey during the sixteenth century along the trade routes that brought it to Europe from the mines in central Asia. The stone passed through Turkey, where merchants traded the stone in bazaars, so it was called "Turkish stone" or, in French, *turquoise.*

The stone was always considered to have more power when combined with an amuletic symbol. For instance, in the desert in Arizona, among the Pueblo de Los Muertos ruins, an amulet in the shape of a seashell was discovered. Encrusted with turquoise, it bore the figure of a toad in the center, which was a sacred emblem of the Zuni people.

Similarly, in Egypt, green-shaded turquoise scarab beetles signifying regeneration were placed on the breast of mummies. Mummification was a common burial practice; it included removing the internal organs before the body was washed and embalmed using palm oils and incense with sweet-smelling preservatives such as cinnamon and spice, mixed with sawdust and beeswax, before the body was encased in a wrapping of linen and placed in the stone or wood sarcophagus. The heart was regarded as the seat of life and was therefore the object of special care following death, symbolically represented by the turquoise scarab. The actual heart was enclosed in a special receptacle, often accompanied by a written prayer, which was buried alongside the mummy. Only after it had been subject to the weighing of the heart ceremony in the afterlife (a heavy heart denoted wrongdoing), could it retake its place in the body of the deceased. As the ultimate goal was to ascend to paradise, everyone was encouraged to live well and thereby die with a light heart.

OPPOSITE Turquoise spheres and pebbles, dark blue chrysoprase pieces, and pale blue crystal rock

At the annual Tucson gem fair, I met with Navajo jeweler Jesse Monongya, who was raised by his grandmother on the Two Grey Hills Reservation in New Mexico. She taught him to tell the seasons by looking up at the position of the Big Dipper in the sky. Her stories of the constellations, shooting stars, turquoise mountains, opal moons, and terraced clouds of gold are reflected in Monongya's mosaic pieces, which use turquoise and lapis lazuli.

Monongya explained the importance turquoise still has for his tribe in rituals and ceremonies: "It's part of our deepest spiritual world; we treat a gift of turquoise like a king, which is why it's always kept in a medicine pouch and we communicate when we pray with crystal." Turquoise is entwined in every stage of Navajo life. At birth a baby receives its first turquoise beads. The stone is also used in puberty rites, weddings, initiation ceremonies, and healing rituals as a guardian of body and soul.

Lapis Lazuli—A Piece of Night Sky

The blue stone called *lapis lazuli* evokes the starry firmament in its natural deep pigmentation and twinkling glints of white and gold. The blue in the stone is lazurite, which combines with white calcite and flecks of golden pyrite that glitter against the dark blue, making the experience of interacting with lapis like holding a piece of the night sky.

Ancient Egyptians used the term *blue stone* to describe the deep celestial shade of lapis, which lies next to indigo on the color spectrum. Pliny the Elder may have been describing the stone when he wrote, "There is a stone called cyanus, of dark blue color, which is sometimes combined with a gold dust." Lapis was transported to Egypt from its only known source in the ancient world, the Badakhshan Province in northeastern Afghanistan. Marco Polo wrote of the beauty of the rock when he visited the country in 1271, describing the "high mountain, out of which the best and finest blue is mined."

Lapis was considered the stone of royalty. It symbolized the sky, the river Nile, divinity, and protection from harm. Egyptian devotion to the color was illustrated by the blue hair of the chief deity of their empire, the god Amun-Ra. This was mimicked on the death mask of Tutankhamun, and the stone was inlaid around his eyes on the mask. Lapis held connotations of truth and mental clarity, so it was frequently shaped into an eye to make a powerful amulet. The eye of Isis, the greatest goddess of life and magic, was said to watch over the dead on their journey into the afterlife.

Some of the oldest examples of lapis were found in Neolithic sites in Pakistan along the ancient trade route between Afghanistan and the Indus Valley dating from the seventh millennium BCE. An abundance of lapis burial ornaments have been found in graves of kings and queens, suggesting the stone possessed an important ritualistic value and godly importwance. The tomb of Queen Pu-abi in the Royal Cemetery at Ur in Sumeria contained her headdress of gold leaves, lapis, and carnelian, as well as artifacts fashioned from lapis lazuli, including cylinder seals, necklaces, hair combs, and statuettes of animals.

The blue of lapis was so popular that from 2500 BCE, ink in that color was manufactured for hieroglyphics and for scribes to write with on papyri, and funerary objects were often glazed in the color. Later, the stone itself was ground and mixed with oils to impart its color to a pigment named ultramarine ("beyond the sea"), so that the blue of the heavens could bring life and light into artworks. We know that women were involved in this creative process because lapis was recently discovered in the dental tartar of a nun buried somewhere between 997 and 1162 CE at a nunnery in Dalheim, Germany. Historians believe she had illustrated manuscripts illuminated in a lapis-based medium, and the stone gradually became engrained in her teeth because she used her lips to lick the brush to a point.

In 1550 BCE, the Ebers Papyrus, the oldest medical papyri of ancient Egypt, describes the use of crystals for healing. The ancients crushed stones and mixed the dust into potions and ointments that were fed or applied to the patient. Emeralds were recommended as a laxative, rubies cured the spleen, amethyst was an antidote to snakebites, while blue sapphires and lapis lazuli were used to heal eye diseases.

The Catherine Palace, near St. Petersburg, Russia, contains great lapis doors, walls, and fireplaces. In similar style today, Dale Rogers provides monolithic marvels of lapis to a new generation of art collectors designing modern spaces. Finding the contemporary art market repetitive, they've turned their attention to seeking rare minerals as unique one-off natural art forms. A few are spiritually minded, but others arrive at Rogers's warehouse accompanied by their lighting expert to measure a piece for a plinth, or an interior designer clasping fabric color swatches to match to the mineral they intend to be the statement piece in the room.

Rogers began his career thirty years ago Indiana Jones–style, fighting for mining rights at the source in Morocco, dealing with local Berbers, and hiring camels and trucks to drag out gigantic slabs from the earth. He was driven by his visualization of the effect that a vast fossil or crystal masterpiece could have on the interiors of a house.

He began offering crystal for sale in London in the late 1970s, from a stall in the Portobello Road Market. At the time it was a tough sell, since interiors were all about chintz and no designer shared his concept. Rogers persevered and was persuasive in his determination that rare natural design would become treasures of the future. He was right. He now serves seventy countries from a vast warehouse glistening with an intriguing array of colossal stones.

On one occasion he returned from Kabul with 550 pounds of lapis, his favorite stone because of the color, which he equates with Klein Blue, the signature color of painter Yves Klein. He's designed some into a *pietra dura* tabletop for his home, where elements of the natural world swamp his sitting room. One vast chunk of rock crystal required two people to lift it onto his desk. Resting on the floor, because no shelf would be strong enough to hold them, are three immense blocks of lapis. "I love blue, but I think it's the zigzags of gold that make it so special," Rogers says. "It really hits your imagination like no other stone." Lapis has been his lucky stone, serving him well on his travels.

Self-Awareness & Self-Expression

Although colloquially we use the word *blue* to imply melancholy or sadness, the blue of lapis—like that of turquoise—is a feel-good color. Remember that sometimes the problems we mull over and worry about have little basis in reality. The "stone of truth," lapis, will help you get honest with yourself. Start an inner dialogue with your stone because it will be a truthful and constructive conversation that carries a positive message. And it can be an enjoyable experience. Lapis will call you out on the excuses you use to keep anxieties intact, and encourage you to take responsibility for what is fundamentally a choice.

Some people find lapis more intense and powerful than turquoise, but both will help with travel anxiety. Imagine them as the eye of Isis, watching over your journey so angst doesn't become your definition. Lapis seeks only affirmative thoughts; when traveling, practice what I call blue-sky thinking, touching your lapis or turquoise frequently to reconnect you with that promise to yourself. Thinking better persuades physical reactions to follow.

Some people I know use rock crystal and lapis together to recharge their "batteries" on arrival. They hold a stone in each hand, one with its points directed at the wrist, the other pointed in the opposite direction.

During a journey I keep a tight grip on a turquoise or lapis stone while thinking of the sheer simplicity and comfort of the journey I'm taking in comparison to what travel entailed for our ancestors. The ancients believed that lapis improved the chances of a cure; that kind of cure is what scientists call the placebo effect and what I refer to as my blue-sky thinking. You want the stone to dispel anxiety? Expect it, and you're halfway to dissipating it.

Remember that anxiety usually has a trigger that makes us feel ill at ease each time we experience it. The phrase "in the unlikely event of a water landing" does it for me every time as I conjure up the freezing waters below when flying in turbulence over the Atlantic at night. (Once, the pilot unhelpfully pointed out that we were flying over the wreck of the *Titanic*. Now that nerve-inducing moment of frantically scanning the map to see how close we are to Greenland in case of an emergency landing is etched in my memory.)

Now, instead of nervously scanning the dark from my cabin window, I examine my fragment of lapis night-sky to stop my mind from wandering and imagining the worst. If you've experienced a traveling trauma, the stone will give you the strength and courage to stop replaying the scenario. We can cope with air turbulence, but when we are emotionally turbulent, our minds are too agitated to reach a peaceful outcome.

With practice, you even might gain the ability to see clearly what is happening in a situation, as opposed to your anxious interpretation of it. And for those who travel constantly and have the rootless, itinerant feeling that comes with it, the stones provide a sense of home and the familiar.

There's no going back; humanity is on the move and we need to acquire the confidence to enjoy journeys to new horizons without carrying the weight of anxiety in our hand baggage. The Greeks and Romans rewarded those who performed feats of bravery with a piece of lapis. Take a lapis or turquoise to watch over you before traveling—or to reward yourself afterward. The choice is yours.

| **ABOVE** Unpolished piece of lapis lazuli

PIPPA SMALL ——— Feeling Safe on the Move

It was a Tibetan turquoise found in Nepal that began anthropologist and activist Pippa Small's journey with stones, which eventually altered her life course. "I was an anthropologist working in Borneo, but the work involved traveling all over Asia, and I began living with constant anxiety," she says.

Small kept her Tibetan turquoise in a small bundle of objects that included her father's St. Christopher charm and a ruby-and-turquoise earring passed down from her great-grandmother. Convinced they would keep her safe, she kept them ready for each journey. "People assumed I had the turquoise with me for religious reasons," Small explains, "but it has a lot of protective qualities when I travel. I find the consistency of it comforting to have by my side, in spite of things coming and going when you're on the move. There's a part of me that feels safer in nature, and the stone is still, ancient, and wise, with a sense of permanence that is consoling."

The landscape, including rocks, were part of human life from the beginning, and somewhere deep inside, Small believes, we hold on to that. These thoughts chime with the principles of animism, which holds that objects, places, and creatures all possess a distinct spiritual essence. "It gives the natural world an emotional life," she continues. "A stone's manifestation as a physical object represents that." In Small's world, stones aren't merely decorative; like her turquoise, they perform a function in our lives.

She prefers to have most stones suspended on wax cords, which can't snap like a chain, so that the stone amulet remains fixed to her and she feels it resting on her skin. The turquoise remains loose in a velvet pouch for the frequent travel she now undertakes for the Turquoise Mountain charity, which is regenerating cultural heritage in such historic areas as Afghanistan, Burma, and the Middle East.

Young Afghanis are learning to cut lapis lazuli, which Small describes as a "soulful" stone. She visits the workshops in Kabul several times a year and is working on a new project with Syrian refugees, but as a mother now of young twins, her level of travel anxiety and apprehension that comes with the risk of visiting dangerous countries has escalated. But her belief in the benefits of this philanthropic work overrules her fear, and with the help of her turquoise—always the first thing she reaches for to pack—her travels continue.

GREEN

malachite & jade

Growing confidence and commitment to dismiss guilt

Even the most talented of us suffer from guilt. Playing an assortment of roles leads to a complicated emotional tug between work and home. Acting as guardian and comforter to children, while being preoccupied and exhausted from work, can lead to feelings of inadequacy. At any age, the repertoire of skills a woman needs to forge the smooth progress of her life has to be enormously varied; we have to assess priorities, which leads to self-reproach when things drop off that day's roster. I know women who feel remorse about unanswered emails, and a sense of guilt can even sneak in when you haven't seen a particular friend for a while. The constant juggling act that makes up our lives today has turned guilt into the default mode of an entire generation.

Malachite—Goddesses' Green Stone

The vibrant green of malachite makes it a powerful ally for anyone trapped by the self-sabotaging feelings of guilt. Malachite's mesmerizing bands can activate the cognitive side of your intellect to help you spot guilt-blocks. While it's a positive to help others, you don't need to take on their emotional baggage; it's enough to own the responsibility of forging yours and your family's life.

In some parts of Italy there's a tradition of wearing malachite pendants, called peacock stones, because they suggest the vibrant green feathers of a peacock's tail. The peacock is thought to confer protection and safeguarding, and you need shielding from the manipulation of a guilt trip.

The beautiful opaque green circles and stripes of malachite are produced from the weathering of copper ores in the stone. Malachite mostly occurs as a thin crust over a host rock with a green streaky texture as opposed to a crystal form. It performs low on the Mohs scale of mineral hardness, only 3 to 4, whereas jade is rated between 6 and 7. Many believe its name

OPPOSITE Green stones bought in a Moroccan market and given to Sheherazade Goldsmith by her son

comes from this quality, from the Greek word *malakos*, meaning "soft." An alternative theory has the name derived from *malacke*, alluding to its color, which resembles the leaf of the mallow plant.

Soft as it is, malachite possesses sufficient strength to bolster commitment to promises that you've made to yourself and others, which lessens the likelihood of guilty feelings. It is also thought to be merciless in exposing your irritating personality imperfections, requiring you to take full accountability for them. To me, malachite looks like a brain with the swirling patterns, making it an apt metaphor for the circular patterns of guilt that spin around in our heads.

OPPOSITE Bathside piece of fluorite and a face-saving jade roller

Last Christmas, my husband gave me a piece of malachite mounted on a stand. I can't explain it, but I knew immediately that I would never bond with it, even though green is my favorite color. Malachite is strong stuff. In Britain we call it the Marmite stone, after the paste made of yeast extract. As with Marmite, there's no in-between with malachite: you either love it or hate it.

Wassily Kandinsky described "absolute green" as "the most anesthetizing color possible." Perhaps that's the reason I found that particular piece of malachite so deadening. In any event, I had to tactfully engineer a return of the stone as soon possible. Of course, returning a gift only replaces it with a perfect little package of guilt. When I found a new malachite that did speak to me, it was smaller, loose, and not set on a high plinth. Was that the reason I didn't bond with the first one?

Guilt is terribly time-consuming. It takes up valuable headspace that we need for thinking about more important matters. When you're obsessing about a guilty feeling, it can pop into your brain about thirty times a day. Even worse, complaining about it shrinks the hippocampus portion of the brain, which is critical to problem solving. Guilt simply isn't good for you.

The Egyptians were the first to make extensive use of malachite. They discovered the stone four thousand years ago in copper mines in hills between Suez and Sinai and those located near Eilat on the Red Sea, often called King Solomon's mines.

Malachite was used to line the headdresses of pharaohs, the idea being that it would raise the wearer's human vibrations so that he could open his mind to receive wise counsel from the spirits. There is a legend that malachite protects the wearer from falling, which possibly originated with ancient Egyptian miners to protect them as they ventured deep within the earth. They bored horizontal shafts, like narrow corridors into the mountain, which

were shored up by massive pillars of the native rock. The work was difficult and dangerous, and the terrain harsh, with no local water supply. Provisions had to be brought by donkey caravan.

Inscriptions on the ruined entrances to old mines and the temples built alongside are dedicated to the miners' spiritual protector, Hathor, mother of the sun god, Ra, and the goddess of light and rebirth. Hathor was the mistress of life, embodying joy and protecting miners as they searched for malachite, copper, and turquoise. She was called Lady of Greenstone—malachite. Miners placed themselves directly under Hathor's protection, found in the swirling patterns of green malachite.

Green, like Hathor, was associated with new life. The ancient Egyptian hieroglyph for the color green was the papyrus stalk, which they held in high regard, and the term for *paradise* was "field of malachite."

ABOVE Malachite, ebony, and rock crystal paperweight by Belmacz

Regeneration & Hope

Beauty was regarded as holiness in ancient Egypt, and cosmetic enhancement was integral to daily life. Archaeologists have found evidence of palettes and grinders for preparing malachite eye paint in tombs, suggesting that the stone was also essential in the afterlife.

The Louvre's collection features fifty kohl pots that were hidden in the heads of statuettes. Some are simple alabaster or rock containers; others are more decorative. Wealthy Egyptians applied around their eyes a thick black kohl, or *kajal*, which was made of finely ground minerals such as galena, a lead sulfide, which was mixed with powdered pearls, gold, emerald, or malachite for subtle color and a shimmering effect. Saffron and frankincense were added for fragrance. A little oil or milk was used to form a paste, which was then painted around the eyes and eyelashes using a feather or finger. Peasants aimed for the same effect using animal fat and soot.

The ancient Egyptians used the word *kohl* for "palette" and "protect," signifying that an unadorned eye was unprotected and therefore vulnerable to the evil eye. Kohl also had the practical purpose of defending the eyes from the blinding sun.

The ancient Egyptians may have realized the malachite-kohl mixture contained another vital form of physical protection. In 2010, French researchers analyzing trace residue in kohl pots proved that the lead chlorides and metallic copper carbonate in malachite produced extra nitric oxide in the eye area, which acts as a disinfectant. The kohl acted as an antibacterial agent, reducing the risk of eye infections from flies, wind-borne sand, and waterborne infections along the Nile, which were common, leading to cataracts and blindness.

The Ebers Papyrus, a text concerning herbal knowledge dating to 1550 BCE, documents that powdered malachite was also ground into a paste to treat wounds and inflammations. It was mixed with raw honey, which heightened the antibacterial effect. This prophylactic effect of malachite was also noticed several millennia later, in the midst of a cholera outbreak in nineteenth-century Paris: copper workers appeared to be immune to the epidemic.

Though copper exposure protected those workers from disease, over the long term the metal collects in the body and becomes toxic. That would have provided another reason for miners to seek Hathor's protection. It is dangerous to cut malachite without protective equipment, since grinding the stone aerosolizes the copper, and the miners would have been inhaling the dust. (Although it's completely safe to handle both rough and polished specimens, it's not a good idea to drill malachite—or any stone for that matter—lest you inhale the dust.)

> "I also made a Medusa head out of malachite that was incredibly complex. Malachite dust is poisonous so it had to be carved using extraction and masks and water."
>
> —DAMIEN HIRST, BRITISH CONTEMPORARY ARTIST

Romans believed that green was restful to the eyes because it was the color of nature and regeneration. Similarly, our modern eyes favor green for its association with peacefulness and hope. Four-leaf clovers and shamrocks proliferate in green stones as bodyguards. In Russian legend, drinking from chalices carved from malachite transferred the stone's powers, and during the early seventeenth century, the fourth Mughal emperor, Jahangir, treasured a collection of about fifty wine cups made of semiprecious and precious gemstones. One that was used in the Mughal royal court as a wine cup featured a hexagonal bowl carved from a 408.5-carat emerald resting on a carved stem.

"Yes, I did drink from it," admits David Warren of Christie's, who auctioned the cup for 1.8 million pounds (about $2.8 million at the time) in 2003. "It was a fun experience, and I did feel emotional. But I didn't notice any special powers coming my way or mind-altering moments. Of course, I was drinking water, and Jahangir would have felt differently because he was known to sip a heady mixture of wine with opium from his wine cups." Quite clearly, Jahangir should have been sipping from amethyst.

Malachite has always been used for large-scale decorative effects; several classical authors refer to fifty-foot columns covered in a green gemstone. According to Pliny the Elder, the Temple to Diana in Ephesus was decorated with malachite.

When large deposits of the stone were found during the nineteenth century in the Russian Urals, the czars flaunted paneling and intricate work in malachite to decorate palaces in monumental forms. The Winter Palace in St. Petersburg, part of the Hermitage Museum, features a stately salon entirely decorated with malachite, arranged in 1830 by Empress Alexandra Feodorovna. The centerpiece is a grand fireplace with an alley of columns alongside. Possibly the motif was chosen because the Romanovs, like many others, believed that malachite was a lucky stone, and this green stone salon was traditionally the room where royal brides dressed for their wedding.

In the ancient cultures, malachite was dedicated to goddesses such as Aphrodite, as well as Hathor, so it's well suited to this peculiarly feminine issue of guilt. Sometimes we lay blame at our own door before anyone else has a chance. Often we think that if we feel guilt, then we surely must *be guilty*.

Use your green stone to decipher if the guilt you feel is merited or not. When guilt behaves like a hungry parasite, depleting your energy, you have to knock it on the head for good. Think of it as a weed that adds nothing to the garden. If you only cut it back, it will rise again. You need to pull it out firmly from its roots.

Jade—Precious Luck

Jade, too, is considered a lucky stone. From the earliest Chinese dynasties until the end of imperial rule, jade was used to ensure luck, good fortune, and protection. Chinese bridegrooms give a jade butterfly to their brides as a symbol of successful love. The tradition arises from an old story of a young man who made his way into the garden of a rich Mandarin in pursuit of a butterfly. Rather than being admonished, the story ended with him marrying the daughter.

"And here, as I found later in Russia, the finest things were not always in possession of the wealthiest, but frequently of the poor; for here the natives dug jade from the ancient graves."

—GEORGE KUNZ, "AMERICAN TRAVELS OF A GEM COLLECTOR"

In another story, jade is said to be the semen of the great Chinese dragon, which solidified after he'd scattered his seed on the earth. Don't let that put you off. Jade's good fortune can shore up reason, preventing guilt from seeping in and spreading its particular poison.

What we call jade can be either of two similar but distinct minerals: jadeite or nephrite. The difference was not recognized until the 1800s. Both are found in a wide range of colors, including green, which is what we are concerned with here. In China, jade amulets are carved in the shape of animals in many different colors, including white nephrite, imperial yellow, and lavender, as well as the more familiar apple green.

Mineralogist and collector George Kunz in a 1927 article made the following observation in the *Saturday Evening Post*:

> The original form of the Chinese character *pao*, signifying "precious," consists of the outline of a house, within which are symbols of jade beads, shell and an earthen jar. This shows that at the very early time when these characters were first used, the Chinese had ready collected jade and employed it for personal adornment.

At one time, the Chinese royal family laid claim to all apple-green and yellow jade, which is how the stone acquired its label of "imperial jade." Even the tombs of a lesser nobleman might yield fifty carved jade amulets and ritual objects. Suits made of jade plaques connected by gold wire were used in the Han Dynasty (206 BCE–220 CE) to preserve the royal body encased within, and jade pieces were placed in the mouths of the dead for protection and safe travels.

The Chinese still believe today that jade will help deal with most of life's difficulties. On a trip to Shanghai, I counted eleven stores of the same jade jeweler along a single street, and one business investor I met said he'd never engage in an important transaction without holding a piece of jade in his hand to protect his interests.

Some women use jade to massage their faces with the aim of attaining a clear complexion and serene visage. In traditional Chinese medicine, *gua sha* refers to "scraping" the skin with a tool often made of jade to improve circulation. The cooling properties of jade pressed against the skin can have an anti-inflammatory effect. Jade can detoxify, and aspects of aging have both psychological as well as physical roots. Pointless suffering, guilt, and angst don't do any of us any favors.

ABOVE Revitilization using green aquamarine and a coral, jade, and rock-crystal earring by Harris Zhu

Rehashing thoughts that arouse guilt keeps you focused on the past. Aldous Huxley, in his preface to the second edition of his dystopian novel *Brave New World*, made the case for letting go of regret:

> Chronic remorse, as all the moralists are agreed, is a most undesirable sentiment. If you have behaved badly, repent, make what amends you can and address yourself to the task of behaving better next time. On no account brood over your wrongdoing. Rolling in the muck is not the best way of getting clean.

Jade was also used as a panacea against mental weakness, and I think we can classify guilt as contributing to such weakness; it can eat away at your mental state so you rarely have a moment's peace. If you made a mistake, allow jade to help you set it right so that you can focus on the present. A guilty setback shouldn't become allowed to blossom into a stumbling block that draws you back into the past.

"There's so much that's outside our control," wrote Gwyneth Paltrow recently in London's *Times* newspaper, "but how do we begin to claim some autonomy over our own health and well being? What levers can we pull that will make a difference to how we feel?"

Jade can be such a lever. Those who believe in its power say it's important to handle the stone so that something of its secret virtue is absorbed into the body (though I wouldn't take this too literally by, say, using a jade yoni egg to strengthen pelvic floor muscles, as recently promoted on Paltrow's website Goop). A round piece of jade can serve as nature's worry ball; roll it around in your fingers as you mentally dismiss the guilt, or place it on your forehead to promote serenity and refocus your mind. It can be near the skin, but keep it outside the body, swinging on a pendant, clipped onto your child's stroller, or placed on a shelf or tabletop in your favorite room.

Of course, if solving issues of guilt and shame were as easy as carrying a small crystal, then everyone in the world would do just that. It takes intention, work, and objective thinking, in addition to the crystal, to change things for the better. Nonetheless, positive stories, case studies, and beliefs passed down about stones endure and new personal experiences add to the "crystal

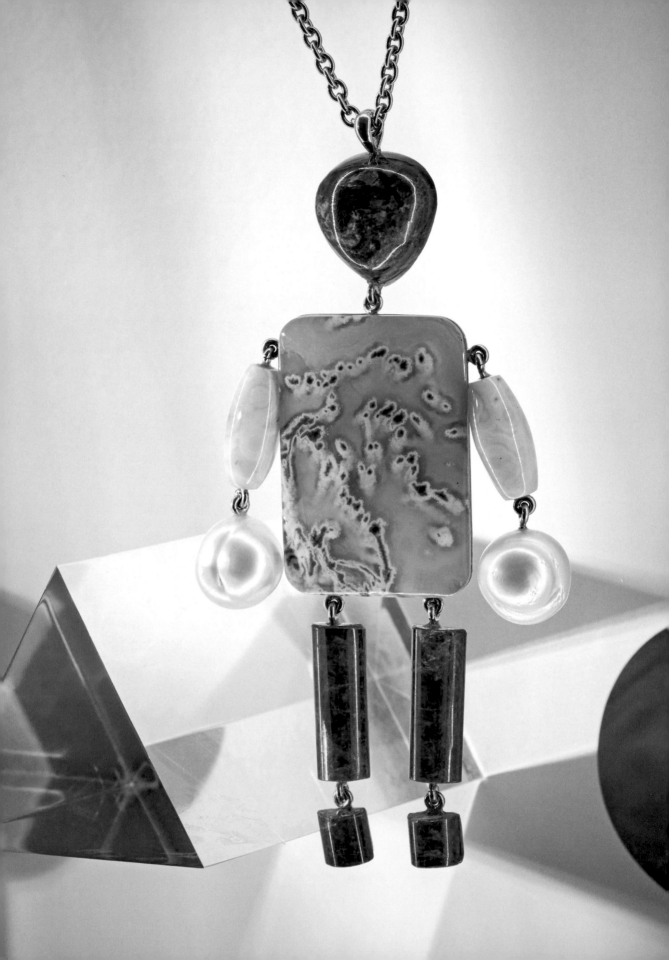

trust" in each new generation. Crystals appeal to universal emotions, and their mood-altering properties can take us to a place that feels a little bit better than where we were before.

Memory & Bravery

The jade of New Zealand defines the story of the native Maori people. The vivid green nephrite, named *pounamu* ("green stone") by the Maori, is found on the South Island of the country's archipelago. It was used for war axes and ceremonial carvings, such as the heirloom pendants called hei-tiki, which depict a human form and serve as memorials for departed ancestors.

These pendants are in the best tradition of a "jewel": the stone, color, symbolism, and design are all imbued with emotion, and having been passed down through an ancient lineage they confer something of the ancestors onto the latest recipient. Descendants feel privileged to wear them when their turn arrives. In cases when the family was dying out, the last male member would leave instructions that the hei-tiki should be buried with him, rather than fall into the hands of strangers.

When American film director and Academy Award–winner Christopher McQuarrie and his wife and producing partner, Heather, together with the cast and crew of *Mission Impossible: Fallout*, visited New Zealand to film a helicopter sequence, they were welcomed by the Maori and presented with jade pendants. "We all wore one," recalls Heather. "They are talismans of strength and protection." Mostly they were carved in *koru* shapes, based on the unfurling silver fern frond, which symbolizes new life and growth, or the masculine *toki* blade, representing strength.

Heather says she has always been aware of jade's aura of good luck, and insists on traveling with what she describes as her "Wonder Woman" Chinese jade bracelets. Her husband tends to run his fingers over a jade rubbing stone when thinking or planning a scene or project. "It's hard to keep track of it sometimes," she says, often wondering "which pair of trousers it's moved into."

In the spirit of the film, she skydived from a plane in tandem with her two children. She tells me the story in a slightly guilty tone, "My mother rang, horrified, to ask if I realized what my children had done. I've done all kinds of crazy stunts—I've either got a brave gene or a stupid one. But something protected me, I'm pretty lucky at this point to be with us."

Heather always buys a stone or jewel at the end of a film project, partly, she explains, because their lifestyle is mobile—moving between film locations, rented homes, hotel rooms, and trailers—and a jade stone is something she can take with her to feel at home. No doubt it also helps assuage any guilt she feels over aerobatics.

If actions are the outcomes of emotions, you can use green stones to regulate how you react to those emotions. Malachite and green jade can settle the feelings in the first instance so you don't make yourself suffer. When you don't know how to deal with anger or fear, you're likely to turn them inward and blame yourself. Guilt is a form of self-torture, depleting your resources, which is bad for your general health.

Sigmund Freud, the founder of psychoanalysis, pronounced guilt as "a most powerful obstacle to recovery." He thought that the primary sources of guilt were fear of authority and the loss of parental love, which make family life the perfect breeding ground for guilt from envy, sibling rivalry, and jealousy. Malachite opens communication channels to help these relationships.

Green is also linked to immaturity, as in a plant's new growth, and malachite supports you to move beyond youthful reactions so that, like a pharaoh listening to wise counsel, you can make mature decisions. And when you're told there is nothing to worry about, and can believe that it's true, there probably isn't.

When guilty feelings are running high, take no action; instead detach yourself from the emotions to look at the situation realistically. Use your green stones to soothe your spirit so that it can find another, more fulfilling, purpose. Rub jade when your feelings are getting out of control and crave a bit of inner peace for yourself to help you feel better.

JADE JAGGER ———— Celebrating Connection

"I've always been attracted to emeralds and jade," says British designer Jade Jagger. "I love buying it in the rough in India, because they bring it to me in large buckets, like dustbins full of sparkling green lumps."

Jagger, the daughter of rock-legend Mick, views the world in color. Initially she wanted to express herself in paint, and she studied at art school, where she created organic paintings of flowers using gold, green, and other strong colors. After a while, though, she felt she couldn't integrate, or compete with other artists. Guiltily, she chucked it in and began to mull over her future. She felt the urge to move on to something more decorative, and realized that throughout her childhood her eye had been groomed to look at stones and jewelry.

"My dad was always into jewelry, mostly antique, and collecting pieces like men's Roman rings," she sasys. "He often bought jewels for my mum, and he'd show them to me when we were traveling."

The first green stone she owned was a small emerald crystal given to her by her father when she was twelve. "Crystals in their natural form give you an energy and elation and absorb your personality into it," she continues. "Now when I'm trading and buying stones in Jaipur, I get that same beat of excitement that I had with my first stone."

Jagger believes strongly that green has a power to connect the mind and has played an important role in her personal life. This is a vital prescription for her modern family, which is increasingly multilayered. Her father has eight children from five different partners, and Jade Jagger delivered her first grandchild when she was nine months pregnant herself. Now her little boy chases around the garden with his niece, who's a month older, and Jagger's latest sibling, a three-year-old brother.

"Jewels and stones might sound superfluous or unnecessary, but they do tie us together and celebrate the unity between people," she says. In her home in the English countryside, she places colorful bowls of emeralds, jade, aquamarines, and rose quartz along her dining table. A large family has more scope for jealousy and competition, but grouped in Jagger's house they communicate and come together. "There's a sense of love," she states. "We try to look after each other, although sometimes we need space, because we do spend ridiculous amounts of time together."

Shortly after they all recently ended a Rolling Stones tour in Prague, Jagger set off for Jaipur with her son Ray to source more jade and emerald support for guilt-free family life.

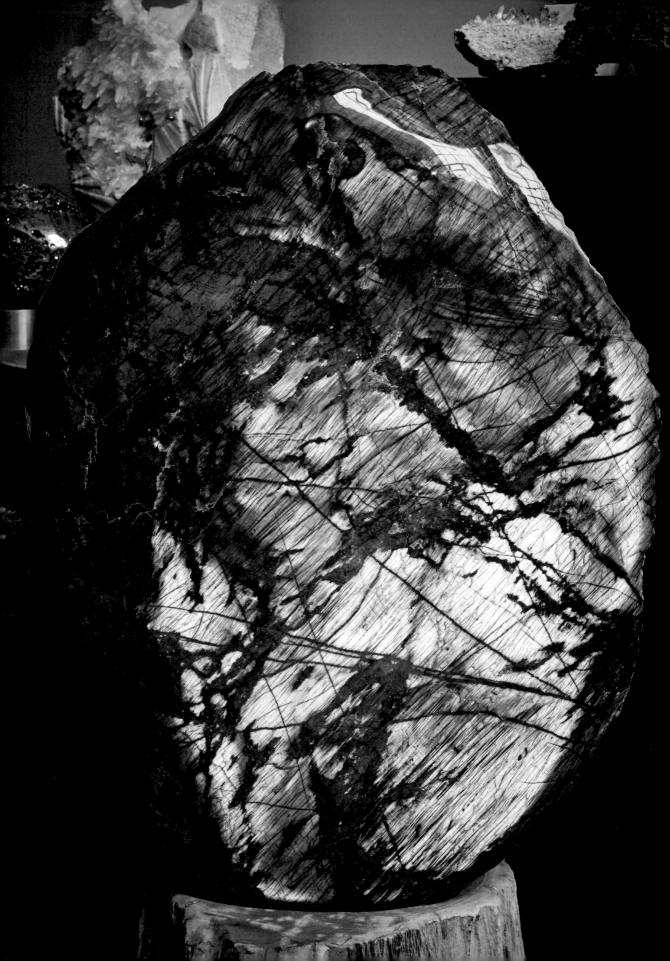

IRIDESCENT

labradorite & moonstone

Fueling strength and wisdom to overcome fear of aging

In our youth-obsessed culture, age is stigmatized, but women pitching themselves against Mother Nature are in a battle we can never win. Each time unflattering candid photos insinuate a model or actress has aged or graphic close-up shots of cellulite play across social media, these insecurities are kept alive.

This isn't a recent phenomenon; women and men alike have been seeking methods of rejuvenation since ancient times. What's different today is how early age anxiety begins to hit, combined with social-media platforms that allow people to present a filtered version of themselves, leading to disappointment when the real-life version doesn't measure up. Society's shifting values mean that many young women's self-perception is now based entirely on their appearance. Hollywood has consistently reinforced the idea that aging is a travesty, and now Instagram has made young women complicit in living the message.

It's life affirming to remember that the ancients respected the principle of the feminine in all her shapes and stages. Actress Jennifer Lopez said recently, in reference to her film *Second Act*, "There's this terrible idea that you get to a certain age and plummet downward. I don't believe that at all. You can always make a change. You can always keep growing. I believe you can keep getting better and better and better."

Labradorite—The Master Stone

Self-mastery is the path to true fulfillment, and the stone labradorite encourages self-discovery. Our states of mind are in flux at every stage of life, older as well as young—we need to constantly change and adapt. Aging is a lifelong process, so consider yourself a work in progress. With the energy of labradorite you can work in harmony with whatever is unfolding for you to discover new potential and possibilities at any age.

We should take inspiration from nonagenarian role models such as Sir David Attenborough and Queen Elizabeth, who travel constantly, work every day, and contribute their efforts to society.

Stone dealer Peter Adler gave me a large pebble of labradorite, which he calls the master stone. I always keep it in my handbag so that whenever I need to I can touch base with the soft green color sparkling with tints of blue, gold, orange, red, and violet. It lends a pleasant feeling when I look at it, and in moments when I might feel demoralized, it helps me see things in a new light.

Labradorite is great for raising the roof on your self-esteem; it acts as the perfect reflector, showing you how you want to be, not what the harsh mirror in the ladies' room tells you. The long-term goal is to raise your confidence level by heightening your energetic makeup so you can get involved in the things that matter to you. It's useful at any age to take stock of where you are in life's cycle, so you can make the most of your possibilities.

Labradorite helps you stop and reflect on what's real and true. It's an iridescent aid to help you face the challenges of living in the present as you navigate schedules, calendars, and plans, which are all about the future. One tip is not to let anything into your schedule without your permission. Often events or meetings slip into our diaries that aren't strictly necessary. Labradorite strengthens your *no* resolve.

Ageing is fine, but an "older" mindset is not. Making an effort or taking a risk can begin to seem terrifying, while sticking to comfort zones and comfortable clothes feels safe—at the cost of making us appear that we've let ourselves go. Nonstop evolution doesn't mean competing with youth's energy or habits; rather, it's the secret to ageing successfully, so you don't feel stuck in a rut or bored. Age is not a barrier to new challenges. It's never too late to take the leap in life to do something you've always dreamed of or confront something or somebody. The good news is that we're living longer and healthier, so we are more capable in mid to later life and can experience more. The old idea that you had one career and then retired belongs to the last century. Age brings skills and experience to new callings, pastimes, and professions.

Wisdom & Fortitude

Labradorite is a feldspar mineral that was first discovered in 1770 on Paul Island in Canada's Labrador Peninsula, which gives the stone its name. Inuit legend has it that the northern lights were imprisoned in rocks along this coastline, which were freed by a blow from a wandering hunter's spear, but a few of the colored sparkles were left trapped within the stone.

Labradorite pieces have been found among artifacts of the Red Paint People, a pre-Columbian culture indigenous to the New England coast. At first glance, some labradorite stones can look an unremarkable grayish green-brown, but when moved slightly the inner brilliance of red and bright green and blue sweeps across the face of the stone. This hidden beauty lies in its molecular structure: practically invisible thin layers refract light back and forth in a display called the schiller effect (*schiller* is German for "twinkle" or "shining"). The effect can only be seen from a specific angle—turn the stone a fraction to the left or right, and the color is lost.

During the nineteenth century, landscape painter William Payne mixed Prussian blue and yellow ochre to make a new shade of gray. It gave the paintings of the time what's termed atmospheric perspective, so that mountains in landscapes appeared to fade into the background with a burst of color peeping through what appeared to be metallic gray mist. This is similar to the phenomenon known in labradorite as labradorescence, which resembles the brilliant display of rainbow iridescence in fish scales or butterfly wings. During the 1960s, French jewelry designer Pierre Sterlé used the stone with great effect in brooches for the heads of birds and their feathered wings.

The stone is softer than quartz, rating 6 to 6.5 on the Mohs scale, and has been carved into cameos; one example of a soldier carved in labradorite lies in the Smithsonian Museum. In 1908, the Prince of Wales bought a necklace composed of labradorite cameos of monkey's heads mounted in gold.

"I wear it when I need something extra," says Emma Askari, laughing as she flashes a pool of labradorite on her finger. "It makes me feel *Game of Thrones* powerful." The adviser to the chairman's office at Christie's auction house and a columnist for *Vanity Fair* Spain, who has sons in their twenties, was impressing on me that she can't live without labradorite. She took a yellow silk pouch out of her bag, splashing drops of rose quartz, tiger's-eye, citrine, and amethyst on the table. They travel everywhere with her, but it's labradorite that she particularly relies on for its colorful depths and feeling of strength.

"I think we communicate through stones," Askari says. "I have a sapphire-and-diamond engagement ring, but it doesn't make me feel as good as my labradorite. Diamonds are too cold; I love my imperfect crystals." She went on to recount stories of women, strangers to her, accosting her to ask about the ring. One explained that she was having a tough time, and Askari invited her to hold the labradorite for a while. The woman did and then hugged her before leaving.

"Something happens," she says, a little bemused, "it's like a magnet. And I suppose some stones do recall the magnetic fields they've come from." This vivacious woman with her inquiring mind, who believes the power of women is necessary to balance the world, is convincing proof that an ageless approach is attractive and compelling. What about the anxiety she does carry? "I'd be petrified to lose one of my crystals, not because of the monetary value but because of what it means to me."

When Askari leaves the restaurant ahead of me, I see the labradorite magic in action. A woman stops her, compliments her chic style, and asks what the colored stone in her ring was. "Just pick a color," she laughs. "Any color you want." She flashed the labradorite in the light and was gone.

Moonstone—Feminine Energy

Moonstones also exhibit the schiller effect; in these stones, it is called adularescence. Moonstone is also a feldspar mineral and thus, like labradorite, can help you accept where you are in time's sequence. In India, the moonstone is considered sacred. Its name in Sanskrit is *candra kanta* (the words mean "moon" and "beloved"), and its powers are thought to be particularly strong during a full moon. Moonstone's reputation glimmers with the moon magic of wise women, fertile mothers, and ancient gods and goddesses. Regarded as the first Victorian detective novel, Wilkie Collin's *The Moonstone* alludes to the stone's power when, after theft, murder, and intrigue, the gem is restored to the forehead of the Indian god from where it was stolen. The moonstone signifies everything spiritually and materially for which humanity strives.

Their close association with the moon lends these opalescent polished pebbles, which glimmer with pastel flashes, an intensely feminine reputation. The length of lunar cycles is closely aligned with those of the female, and both symbolize the repeating rhythm of time. They can enhance the intuitive side of the mind. Time is a natural fact of the universe. Nothing can stop it, so rather than fight, stand your ego down. Enjoy the lifelong adventure, because at each juncture something new and surprising can arise. There's a big world out there and much to learn and master; your moonstone's schiller beams can help you alight on a new experience—something new and exciting at any stage or age.

In Japan each autumn, Tsukimi parties are held in which the moon plays a central role. During these moon-viewing gatherings, which originally celebrated the fall harvest, offerings are made in the light of the full moon. Four hundred years ago at the Katsura Imperial Villa in Kyoto, a bamboo platform, like a high extended veranda, was erected for optimal viewing of the moon during autumn.

1 Strong pieces of labradorite

2 Geometric-shaped fluorite

3 Smoky-quartz pebbles

4 Slices of labradorite carved as ammonite

5 Flat tablet of jadeite

When I visited Kyoto, I was struck by the beauty of the Jojuin Moon Garden at the Kiyomizu-dera temple complex, with Mount Otowa in the background. Burnt orange, yellow, and red leaf-sparks from autumn foliage flashed in the moonlight. The moon transformed the garden: stonewashed arrangements of pebbles glowed ethereally between the silhouettes of mossy hillocks and cloudlike topiaries that surrounded a still pond. The blend of garden and opalescent hazy twilight was what made it magical—separately, they would not have had the same effect. Moonlight connects us to our own luminous center, so the moon has long been a symbol of inner enlightenment. For over six hundred years, the garden has encouraged visitors to reflect and explore their inner landscape.

I've tried to re-create something of the same effect in my garden at home. Electric lights in the city pollute moonbeams, but I've "planted" soft lights at the back of my garden that make the labradorites and moonstones in my terra-cotta pots glitter. Pliny the Elder declared that moonstone changed according to the moon's phases, its brilliancy increasing toward the full moon. My moonstones definitely disperse brighter flashes of pink, orange, and blue under my moon-substitute garden lanterns.

Young Lebanese designer Noor Fares likes to play with lights and the flow of energy from iridescent stones such as labradorite and moonstone in Prana collection designs. The name is derived from the Sanskrit, meaning "breath of life." Fares chooses each healing gemstone to chime with one of the seven chakras, and she subscribes to the Indian belief that the stones should be in contact with the skin, so the backs of the mountings are left open. Long lapis earrings reach the throat chakra, while slices of rose quartz shimmering with the visual effect of layered mother-of-pearl and rock crystal touch the heart. A labradorite pendant is engraved with the symbol of a lotus petal in enamel to correspond to the second chakra, *svadhistanha*, to help the relationship with the self. Fares associates the latter with flexibility and a joyful appreciation of the different aspects of life as you age.

Fares works surrounded by pyramids and spheres of rock crystal and amethyst caves, explaining that she feels more grounded when she's around crystals. Fares cherishes the ritual of occasionally collecting her stones into a basket and leaving them on her balcony for a full-moon cleanse. When we met, she was heavily pregnant with her first child, and like any prospective new mother was full of trepidation about the unknown and what the future held for her and her baby. Although raven-haired, clear-skinned Fares had barely turned thirty, becoming a mother was for her a sign, if not of aging, at least of advancing into the next stage of life. She's drawn to stones with light within them and credits the moonstone for giving her clarity to prepare her for the new phase of parenthood.

OPPOSITE Labradorite, moonstone, and opal jewelry hung on selenite in the studio of Eugenie Niarchos

The Romans dedicated the moonstone to Diana, the goddess of the moon, believing it bestowed the gift of second sight or prophecy. As we traverse natural rhythms and transformations, whether it's childbirth, puberty, or any change-of-life issue, moonstones can calm emotions and behavior.

During the Middle Ages, moonstone was traditionally used to calm the soul and prevent lunacy—until modern times, menopausal women were often thought to be suffering from a type of hysteria (a word that comes from the Greek word for uterus). And although the symptoms of menopause can be extensive, including irritability, depression, loss of confidence, and lack of sleep that can make you feel as if you're losing your sanity, a walk with moonstone or labradorite can help restore your faith in the necessity of life changes. Menopause can be a positive phase associated with newfound freedom and status. Recall that travelers used moonstone for protection—possibly the tiny flashes of light illuminated the way for them in the dark. If that's the case, then we can use it to navigate our way into the next stage of life.

Liberation & Perspective

Around the turn of the twentieth century, moonstones became popular in the art nouveau period. Artists used stylized images of nature in flowing curvilinear designs, incorporating motifs of roots, buds, seedpods, tulips, sunflowers, lilies, wilting poppies, and peacock feathers. Practitioners of the style were committed to abolishing what they perceived as the hierarchy of the arts, in which art and sculpture were viewed as superior to craft-based decorative arts. Master jeweler René Lalique and his contemporaries contributed to an ideological change in jewelry by embracing feminism. This is visible in Lalique's dragonfly women and other winged females, who were symbolically emerging from their chrysalises and flying toward liberation in the new century. Moonstones manifested this spirit of metamorphosis. Precious stones had subsidiary roles in these artistic pieces in favor of translucent and ethereal labradorite and moonstone, which were ideal to highlight the sensual and dreamlike creations. The pearly sheen of moonstone was set in a repertoire of natural scenes to create rays of light, shimmering water, or the moon, evoking seasonal transformations as well as feminine change.

The dream sequences of our lives rarely play out as planned, but there is always happiness to be found in reality as long as it's not killed by disappointment. Look for the schiller effect in all aspects of your life by viewing everything from a slightly different angle, and the glowing rays of positivity can become visible. If you're really not happy with your current life, when the children are launched is the perfect time to risk a change. Identify one exciting goal to explore that might lead to greater happiness and life purpose. And be sure to consult your labradorite from time to time to remember that worth is not dependent on achievement.

Place a moonstone over your heart or solar plexus when you're at home, or wear one on a pendant, and focus on clearing your mind and senses to ease any emotional trauma about advancing years. Like labradorite, it can help banish the fear of moving through a transformational time. The ability of these stones to alter their colors at the slightest tilt will inspire your own flexibility in the way you view and maneuver your future.

Remember that with each cycle of life, your self-knowledge increases, and with wisdom comes power. You'll be able to see beyond the odd wrinkle to perceive the benefits of your years and nurture respect for what you've achieved so far. Labradorite makes an excellent companion for a balanced response to the constant state of flux and change, particularly as you open new chapters.

Labradorite and moonstone can unhook us from the anxiety about lifestyle and looks so that we can cherish what we have gained. I love dancing but always hated nightclubs; aging means I don't feel pressured to step inside one again. Savor some of the benefits. It's liberating not to care what other people think about you the way you did when you were twenty and forever teetering on the edge of uncertainty. With that insight you can weather crises better and dump the notion that you have nothing left to offer.

BELOW Carefully place a smooth labradorite pebble on your forehead to quiet a busy mind

Life remains a voyage of self-discovery, and the adventure doesn't have to stop. Little drops of frozen moonlight illuminate the big changes of a lifespan. Being content with yourself and where you are is the goal. But don't forget to try something new each day if you can—a food that you haven't tried before or a form of technology you've been scared to tackle. (Data shows that people over forty, especially women, start the most successful businesses.) Follow that passion you put away for a rainy day.

Using these stones, we can discard the tunnel vision often associated with aging and see all our possibilities. Actress and model Brooke Shields, now in her midfifties, says she's in better shape than ever. She's a role model for the new tribe of women who refuse to accept traditional middle age and are ready for a new adventure. There's no need to dim your lights at any age, and labradorite and moonstone will push you to shine brightly. These stones are about feminine power, so spread your wings, embrace your age, and fly.

JULIA CONDON ——— Aging Without Limits

Thirty years ago, successful portrait and still-life artist Julia Condon found that crystals transformed her life, as well as the subject matter of her art. "Working with crystals and working with your intuition means you live in a very different way," she tells me. "I try to live through my heart and not my mind. Everything comes from inside, and you can access your joy and give it out. I'm interested in being a powerful woman, to live life fully. I find I get smarter and more experienced as I get older, so this is a good time to work."

Inspired by Renaissance artists such as Titian and Leonardo da Vinci, Condon attended London's Chelsea College of Arts and Central Saint Martins art school before moving to New York to work full-time as an artist assistant and portraitist. In 1985, she began studying meditation, and during a metaphysics class was asked to choose a crystal to work with. She picked up a rock crystal and instantly felt a buzz of energy expanding around her, like a vibrating bubble. This experience inspired her to begin amassing her own collection of crystals, such as moonstone to represent water, amethyst for air, ruby for fire, and emerald for the earth. "I've carried these four stones all over the world. I'd chant holding each stone to bring out the guardian of that element," she recalls.

Gradually she expanded her painting technique into a new oeuvre of abstract and still work, including lifelike paintings of amethyst stones built up in layers of oil, rendering the image from the inside out. Complicated geometrical mandalas followed, which mimic a crystal's internal structure, as she explored working with energy and light. "I never had to figure them out mathematically; they just came out like this," she says. It takes Condon roughly a year to complete one of these complicated pieces of sacred floating geometry, which look like intricately colored kaleidoscopic images. When she completes one, she affixes a tiny crystal imbued with her energy to the back of the canvas.

While living in New York, she began exploring an idea of creating three-dimensional expressions of light and energy by constructing mobiles from glass and crystal (see page 224). (see page 224) "I broke a ton of things to start with, because they would fall off and the mobiles would crash. It had a lot to do with patience and the art of balance," Condon says. She uses smooth crystal beads and hexagonal shapes of mouth-blown glass in complicated weblike patterns. She has to find the equilibrium of the totality, like weighting dozens of scales simultaneously, to balance the structure. In the center of the mobile she hangs an illuminated orb, like the moon, which sends rainbow lights bouncing from the labradorite, moonstone, rock crystal, coral, amber, and jade beads.

After twenty years in the United States, a few years ago Condon made the brave move to Tintagel in Cornwall, in the far southwest of England. She picks up crystal there near Merlin's Cave, named for the wizard of Arthurian legend, which lies below a craggy head of land on which Tintagel Castle stands. Large hunks of blue celestite and pyramids of rock crystal are arranged in her sitting room and bedroom, and bowls of moonstone, labradorite, opal, and agate sit at the base of one of her mandalas. Beneath the studio where she works is a grid of twenty-five colored crystals.

Condon recently turned sixty, and she's busier than ever, traveling, accepting commissions, and bursting with joie de vivre. "It's outside of our culture to enjoy getting older," she says, "but it's actually easier as we age."

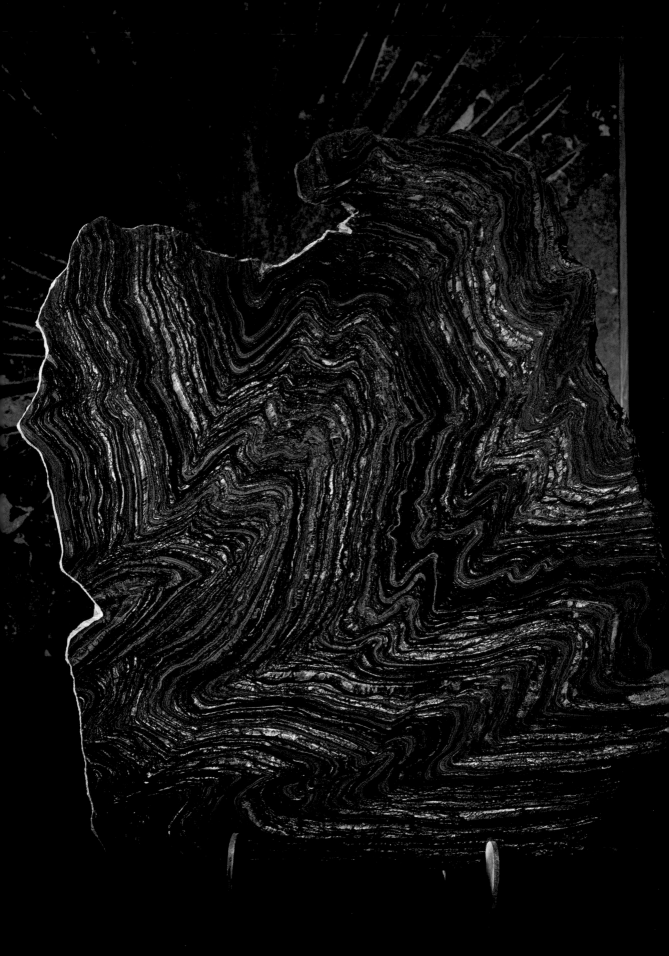

BROWN

tiger's-eye

Achieving balance and insight to strengthen boundaries

COLOR SPECTRUM:
Sunburned-brown quartz
with golden stripes

FOUND: South Africa;
India; Burma; Australia;
Brazil; Canada; and
Arizona, Montana,
and California in the
United States

I'm not sure if my parents knew tiger's-eye was called the stone of independence when they brought one back for me from South Africa. At age twelve it was my first crystal, and I thought it was so exotic, shimmering with energetic gold shafts of light from its stripes. That's what I love about the crystals I've collected over the years, like the celestite pebble from a Scottish rock shop in St. Andrews or the sliver of agate carried back from India. They pull my thoughts back to a certain moment more vividly than any photograph. My tiger's-eye reminds me to clearly and calmly stand my ground.

Tiger's-eye makes a good choice for a young girl because it teaches us the lessons of boundaries and the right use of power, vital in later life to protect ourselves and to resist the urge to say yes to everything. When I sit with women friends, I hear tales of how they take on the lion's share of duties and assume responsibility for things they haven't asked for. Their limits constantly fluctuate between what they will and won't accept from others. It's hardly surprising that our struggle with boundaries is a lifelong journey.

Fortunately, I still have my tiger's-eye to help me maintain my boundaries, and when I feel an uncomfortable tug inside that I'm moving away them, I disengage and work with my tiger's-eye to figure out what's going on with me and the situation at hand.

A Means of Accepting Paradox

Brown was long considered a lowly color, associated in our minds with wood and dirt. And brown or natural-colored clothing paints a humble picture. Brightly colored dyes were expensive before the invention of synthetic colors, and sumptuary laws in many places ensured that only the upper classes could possess colorful fabrics, so status and rank were immediately visible. Those in menial occupations, and even the growing middle class of merchants and skilled craftsmen, were condemned to life in brown.

OPPOSITE Tiger iron with bands of tiger's-eye, haematite, and red jasper displayed at Dale Rogers alongside an agate sphere and a bowl of septarian concretion

Werner's Nomenclature of Colors, adapted in English in 1814 by painter Patrick Syme, was used by young English naturalist Charles Darwin in his survey work aboard the HMS *Beagle* on its voyage around the world. In the book, brown is descriptive of shades from the natural world. Tiger's-eye is a blend of the head of a pintail duck, the breast of a red grouse, the light brown middle part of feathers on a pheasant, and the hazel versions on the back of a snipe. Syme's details are as precise as possible to bring alive the hues imagined on the back of a wild bird, camouflaged as a brown smudge, flying through woods and moorlands. Essentially, brown is a noble color, symbolic of survival in nature and the soil from which we grow our food. Without brown, we wouldn't survive, which arguably gives it a value far above rainbow shades.

A natural clay pigment called *ochre* was likely the first paint employed by humans. In prehistoric body painting and subsequently cave art, such as that at Altamira, Spain, brown ochre, as well as red and yellow, was used on walls and ceilings to depict deer, bison, horses, and other animals, as well human handprints. In South Africa's Blombos Cave, archeologists have found a seventy-three-thousand-year-old design on a stone flake made with an ochre crayon. An abalone shell lined with traces of ground ochre, charcoal, and seal bone to add fat to the mixture was also discovered, which could have made an early painting kit.

In Egyptian statues of deities, brown tiger's-eye was used to represent the eyes. They expressed divine vision, the all-seeing, all-knowing eye. Enhancing the protection provided by the sun god, Ra, and one of the earth gods, Geb, the tiger's-eye was believed to give the gods the ability to observe everything even through closed doors. As Geb was the god of mines and caves, Egyptians believed he supplied the minerals and precious stones in the earth.

In Eastern mythology, the tiger (not the lion) is the king of beasts, so wearing tiger's-eye denoted courage, integrity, and a right to power. Similarly, Roman soldiers wore tiger's-eye amulets into battle to confer courage and deflect opponents' weapons. When the stone is tilted, a golden spark radiates, which was deemed similar to the flash in the eye of a tiger spotting its prey. The hope was that a similar unwavering focus and determination would be transferred to the soldier via the stone and that the flash might distract the enemy.

A friend recently told me that she was taking her tiger's-eye along for confidence on a blind date. Like a Roman soldier, she wanted to focus as she assessed her potential new partner. And, of course, it was also important to maintain boundaries on a first meeting.

ABOVE "Ball crusher" paper weight with a Septarian concretion sphere and a tiger's-eye ring on a black-ened bronze finger, by Solange Azagury Partridge

Not everyone trusts tiger's-eye so blindly. My Pilates teacher won't have one in the house because it brings up unpleasant feelings for her. "It keeps pushing my boundaries," she complains. If you find the vibration of tiger's-eye too strong for you, try another specimen; the energy of raw and polished stones flows differently.

For anyone who is going through a divorce, tiger's-eye would help, because it's a stone of balance, allowing one to see both sides in a negotiation. With tiger's-eye you can embrace paradox by holding contradictory ideas in nonjudgmental acceptance.

Energy & Connection

A member of the quartz family, tiger's-eye displays an optical phenomenon called chatoyancy, in which a band of light like the narrow iris of a cat's eye appears in the pebble. Although there is no opalescence in tiger's-eye, the tawny golden bands do have a silky luster. There is a rare natural red version of the stone called ox eye or bull's eye, and a blue one that is often referred to as falcon's eye or hawk's eye. During the 1800s, tiger's-eye was more precious than gold in South Africa. It could be worn only by tribal leaders and warriors, who displayed it in neckpieces with beads, bones, and shells.

I once sent an email to fashion designer Victoria Beckham's office to ask which crystal she recommends to get through the festive yet exhausting season of parties and looming deadlines. "Tiger's-eye," pinged the reply. "It energizes the body and rebalances on all levels. It fuels courage and strength, and will help you achieve your dreams." It's a good tip to start the day with the coffee-colored rays of tiger's-eye flickering with energy rather than an espresso. The gold band can touch the deepest part of our minds, inspiring enthusiasm, while the brown makes that vital connection to the earth.

Beckham has spent years reading and listening to recommendations from friends to gain her understanding of the power of crystals. She carries black obsidian everywhere, sometimes swapping it for white howlite to calm mind and body when she's stressed. Often, she carries a small collection of different crystals in her handbag. She also likes to share crystals with customers. "We clipped crystals onto belt loops and included secret pockets for them on wide-leg trousers, so you can carry charms where you go," she says. "I want my customer to feel confident and secure and offer her something that could provide support navigating her career and personal life."

Whether it's at the school gates or in a new business situation, we need to sharpen our senses so that we can be alert to details and sum up situations quickly. Think of the Romans undertaking territorial defense by patrolling their fortifications and stone barriers. You can't necessarily take people or things at face value; characters who come into your life need to be sized up, and if you don't pay attention properly, that's when someone will cross a boundary line.

Studies show that those around us influence our thinking and behavior—a friend getting divorced can increase our own risk of a separation. Use tiger's-eye to ensure good connections with the right people and keep them in our lives. If we're honest, we all know we have one or two friends who suck energy out of us and bring negative traits to the table. Use tiger's-eye to spot them and keep them firmly on the right side of your internal barrier. And in any negotiation at home or in the office, tiger's-eye will help protect boundaries—ensuring both parties are satisfied they have achieved what they needed.

Equilibrium & Gravity

In the wild, tigers are a vital part of a boundaried system, helping to keep their environment healthy. They prey on herbivores such as deer that might otherwise overgraze and damage the land, disrupting the balance of the local environment. In a similar way, you can use tiger's-eye to keep track of situations with an open mind and unprejudiced views, which is helpful to solve conflict. Like the tiger, you will be helping to keep your surroundings in a healthy state.

We all encounter many contradictory riddles and complex gray areas in our lives, and tiger's-eye can teach us the balance between extremes, fostering an understanding of how to make an agreement between opposites. Tiger's-eye can be used in any area that helps your capacity for reasoning and compassion. For example, hold a tiger's-eye over your power center just below your heart when looking for a harmonious outcome between two opposing views. The stone helps restore the balance of power in relationships, so you can become your own mediator.

It could be tiger's-eye's properties of conciliation, mental diplomacy, and ability to reach the center ground with no judgment that has made it a favorite stone for Buddhist mala bracelets. The Sanskrit word *mala* means "garland." For thousands of years, Buddhists have wreathed necks or wrists with bands of 108 crystal beads, which they silently pass through their fingers to quiet the mind or to count the number of times a mantra has been recited, a breath taken in during meditation, or the Buddha's name repeated.

1 Boundary-setting smooth tiger's-eye

2 Rough tiger's-eye necklace by Pebble London

3 Banded, mottled, and patterned landscape jasper

4 Agate cave

5 Pebbles of pyrite

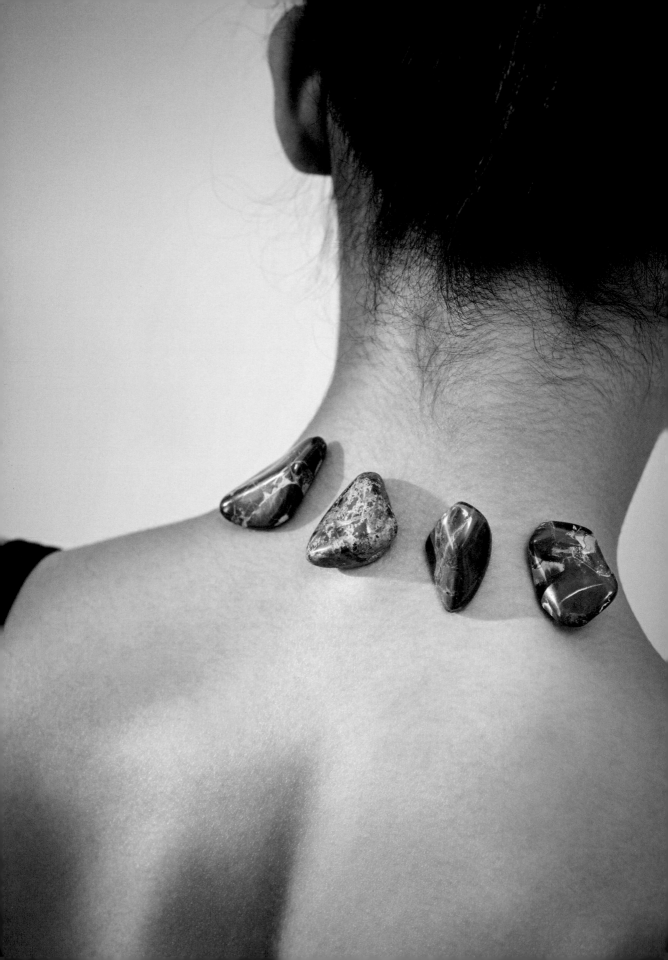

OPPOSITE Dappled brown
nuggets of jasper

Buddhist texts and manuscripts contain numerous references to crystals in conjunction with the mantras used to invoke power during prayer.

Om mani padme hum is the most widely known Tibetan mantra; it translates as "the jewel is in the lotus." A common motif in Buddhism, the lotus symbolizes growth from the soil to blossom, and the jewel references enlightenment. The spiritual leader of Tibetan Buddhism, the Dalai Lama, who wears tiger's-eye beads in his own mala, says this about the mantra:

> Om symbolizes the practitioner's impure body, speech and mind. . . . The path is indicated by the next four syllables. *Mani*, meaning "jewels," symbolizes the factors of the method—the altruistic intention to become enlightened compassion and love. The two syllables *padme*, meaning "lotus," symbolize wisdom. Purity must be achieved by an indivisible unity of method and wisdom, symbolized by the final syllable *hum*, which indicates indivisibility.

Tiger's-eye, too, has been used to allow you to become "invisible" by helping you see through dark situations and your doubt, so that you can negotiate your way out of the shadows with ease and safety. It's an interesting choice of stone for the Dalai Lama to use during his sixty years in Dharamsala, India, where he's set up a democratically based government in exile.

Tiger's-eye isn't the only crystal used for *mala* beads; they are created from nearly every stone found under the earth. (Buddhists favor amethyst beads for meditation *malas*, as they believe the stone is sacred to Buddha.) The stone is drilled and cut into cubes, and then the corners are rounded before the pieces are placed into mills that gradually grind the bead to the correct size and shape. Finally, the beads are polished in rotating drums.

In the *Vogue* office, everyone was tired as we neared the Christmas break. I noticed that beauty director Jess Diner had a red tiger's-eye from her crystal box out on her desk, a stone that allows you to tackle the day in a calm and inspired fashion. A small bottle labeled BALANCE sat beside it, shining with tiger's-eye and quartz gemstones mixed with evening primrose and rosewood oils and jasmine extract; Diner spritzes it liberally on her pulse points. I recalled that someone had told me tiger's-eye helps purify the body after rich food, which makes another good reason to carry it during the indulgent holiday season.

Tiger's-eye's most recent height of popularity was during the 1970s—a time of social and cultural change and transformation, which shaped modern times. Women gained more freedom and personal liberation, and rebellion against authority was a key theme. Fashion took the hippie style of 1960s flower children and transformed it into low-slung flared jeans, fringe, and lots of beads—including tiger's-eye—for young people from all social backgrounds. It sparked a new outlook of individuality, which is about being genuine, erecting a new set of boundaries for a younger generation.

I was drawn to a pair of tiger's-eye earrings when I visited jewelry designer Noor Fares. The radiance of the golden-brown globes was real and palpable. I took this as a sign that I needed to use my tiger's-eye at this busy time. My thoughts were scattering, and the stone would help me corral them so that I could make sense of them. I was in discussions for a new project and needed unwavering focus. We can't make decisions from an emotional platform, and I needed to understand the different viewpoints.

No one can keep our personal boundaries intact better than we can. Furthering our own interests while balancing our needs with those of others is a specialty of tiger's-eye. If tempers begin to flare, reach for tiger's-eye to regain composure and restore equilibrium. The brown energy of the stone can ground and stabilize even if everything around us may be erupting into chaos. Tiger's-eye reminds us that anger can make for a swift solution, but when we face problems with compassion and sincerity and positive motivation, our solution will ultimately be better—even if it takes longer.

This stone is about vivacity and inner strength and confidence to protect where you lay your outer parameters and borderlines for others to respect. To boost your personal will, carry rich, earthy tiger's-eye when boundaries are looking vulnerable and lack of confidence is on the prowl.

ALEXANDRA JEFFORD ———— Listening to the Heart

At age twelve, Alexandra Jefford was at her parents' home in Geneva when a painting inexplicably fell off the wall onto the floor, shattering the glass. The painting, created by a family friend, depicted trees surrounding the Worcestershire English country home of her grandmother, Isobel.

Jefford says, "I immediately thought my grandmother was dead, although there was no reason for me to think that at all, or any forewarning. All I can say is that in my heart, I felt it. I knew, God knows how, but that was my train of thought." It was unclear why the painting had fallen, since the cord hadn't broken and the nail was still in the wall. Shortly after, Jefford learned her grandmother had died.

Now a ceramicist and designer, Jefford had spent every summer as a child with Isobel in the garden tending her rose beds and kitchen garden. "I really missed her when she went. I adored my grandmother to bits. She was smart and soft, and everything around her was beautifully crafted," Jefford recalls.

Another strong memory she has of her grandmother was the oval tiger's-eye ring from the 1970s that Isobel always wore. "It was the first piece of jewelry that I remember as a child. It was a powerful memory, and I only associated tiger's-eye with my granny," she says. Although Jefford loved the link of the stone with her grandmother, she'd never owned the stone herself—until recently.

When Jefford's yoga instructor was traveling to Japan, she gave him a piece of black tourmaline from an assortment of crystals that she keeps in a bowl in her office to travel with. In return, when he came back from his travels, he gave her a *mala* bracelet of tiger's-eye beads he had chosen for her. As it happened, it was two days before Jefford's birthday. On her way home, she ran into an acquaintance who's always professed to have physic abilities. The woman pulled Jefford aside, saying she had to deliver an urgent message. "Your grandmother has asked me to tell you she's sent you a birthday present," the woman said, looking bemused. "I don't know what it means, but I had to tell you."

Jefford wears the tiger's-eye bracelet a lot, and keeps it with her in her handbag when it isn't on her wrist. "What my friend said can't have just been pulled out of a hat after all this time," she maintains. "It's too weird; there has to have been something . . . somewhere."

The tiger's-eye is a tangible memory of her beloved granny and reminder of the cyclical nature of life, which helps her maintain boundaries in terms of how she'd like to live and what achievements she'd like to make. "If that's the purpose it serves, then it's a good thing," says Jefford.

WHITE

selenite

Using moon magic and cleansing to defeat self-doubt

COLOR SPECTRUM:
Ice-cube clear to white
satin and pearl

FOUND: Mexico, Morocco,
New Mexico, and Oklahoma
and New York in the
United States

Selenite connects you to your angel guide who'll bring a divine light into everything she touches. Two friends of mine related an experience about stepping onto dewy grass in Millbrook, New York, to meditate in the moonlight with their selenite wands. They focused on meeting their spirit guides and guardian angels. Apparently, you can receive advice in the form of "interior movies"; words aren't used, but a symbolic story is told. "Well, it was a bit like *Pride and Prejudice*," one of the friends told me the next day. "The pictures I saw seemed to tell me Selene was blessing my new romance," referring to the Greek goddess of the moon.

With a sweep of the wand, you can be cleared of any unwanted energy prompted by the gremlins of self-doubt. Negative thinking makes us underestimate our abilities and subsequent performances. Using selenite can feel almost spiritual, as the wand carries intentions to the higher self and beyond. Holding the selenite above your head sets it to the task of unlocking the blockage of self-doubt to allow a freer flow of energy.

Because selenite encourages connection with the wise feminine divine power, it is a useful stone to have around during female rites of passage, when self-confidence can feel depleted with hormonal shifts. The calcium and sulfur base of the stone stimulates the emotional body, compelling you to move forward and leave the stagnant pool of uncertainty behind.

Lucidity & Fertility

Selenite takes its name from the Latin *selenites* and the Greek *selēnitēs lithos*, which translates as "stone of the moon." The stone's luster evokes moonlight; it glows ethereally, like alabaster. Some pieces have a clear or glasslike appearance, while others look fibrous, with dendrites or fossils inside. Desert rose is a variety of selenite with a russet-brown color, from the ancient desert sand where it's found in Mexico and Morocco.

OPPOSITE Magnificent selenite fireplace set into Robert Procop's Sunset Boulevard living room

In Mexico, selenite grew in vast subterranean caves for hundreds of thousands of years, taking tabular, reticular, or columnar shapes. In 2000 CE, two brothers opened a new tunnel in the Naica silver mine in southern Chihuahua, looking for a new vein of precious metal. Instead they discovered what are thought to be the largest crystals on planet Earth. John F. Ross wrote in *Smithsonian* magazine about the discovery:

> Deep below the surface of an isolated mountain range in Mexico sit two rooms of splendor; translucent crystals the length and girth of mature pine trees lie pitched atop one another, as though moonbeams suddenly took on weight and substance.

Two cathedral-size chambers contain crystals measuring up to forty feet long and a yard wide. The smaller Cave of Swords was discovered in 1910 and explored extensively (and damaged by foot traffic and exposure to air). Only a handful of people have ventured into the recent discovery, the Giant Crystal Cave, which lies almost a thousand feet beneath the surface. The temperature there hovers at well over 100 degrees Fahrenheit, with 90 to 100 percent humidity.

The first American woman to have visited the cave and photographed the crystals is author, explorer, and healer Leela Hutchison. Exploring the larger, deeper cave meant crawling over the gargantuan translucent crystals in pitch black with only a miner's light on her helmet to guide her. In this hostile environment, she could stay in the cave only for minutes at a time before becoming disorientated. Her blood thinned quickly and she constantly cinched in the belt holding her battery pack because she lost water so rapidly, and the risk of fainting from heat exhaustion was a real probability.

In spite of the danger, Hutchison found the experience mind-expanding. "I felt I had been knocked down by a tsunami of energy. I felt altered beyond words. I had no foreknowledge that the photos I took would be the start of a new chapter of passionate purpose in my life," she exclaims.

Hutchison's visit to the caves was followed by years of learning. She felt propelled to become a gemologist in order to speak clearly about the crystals in a scientific way as well as to relate the impact they'd had on her.

"I was humbled by what I saw; the crystals changed my life and enhanced everything I did," she says. She keeps selenite at home for its ever-flowing white light as a beacon of clearing to enhance the room, and she has become selenite's busiest ambassador, delivering talks about her experience around the world. Presciently, Hutchinson described the first sight of giant crystals akin to entering "Superman's Fortress of Solitude." There was no kryptonite, but now we know there was alien life in the caves, which had

Carved selenite book ends

been slumbering for tens of thousands of years within the giant crystals. NASA's Astrobiology Institute director Penelope Boston and her team took samples of microbes from pockets of trapped fluid, which had adapted to survive the extreme conditions within the caves, discovering microbial life forms that are genetically distinct from anything previously known on Earth. Were Selenite's moon and otherworldly magic at work?

The color white broadly symbolizes purity and cleanliness. Swiss French architect and painter Le Corbusier recommended whitewashed interior walls to act as a moral and spiritual cleansing for society, and white has become the color of power for minimalists and visionary modernists such as Japanese architect Tadao Ando and Britain's John Pawson.

Modern Mexican healing treatments use quartz prisms and white selenite swords of light to align the spirit, eliminating self-doubt while you relax. Gender activist and model Munroe Bergdorf, the first transgender woman featured in a L'Oréal Paris campaign, wears crystals in her clothes in a strict rotation of stones, including selenite. She told *Vogue*, it is "to help me through transitional periods and lift my spirit." She sometimes walks the runway with a rose quartz tucked in her pocket.

Author and crystal healer Emma Lucy Knowles, who works with Victoria Beckham, has gleaming selenite in many forms around her home. "I have the most amount of selenite in the sitting room for calm, and my bedroom, to help me sleep, as it's very protective," she says. "I have selenite lamps and a sphere. It gives my house an angelic feeling, which is very nurturing. It's almost like it's from another planet, it's so uplifting."

For twenty years, Knowles worked for a media company by day and burned the midnight oil studying and working with crystals—nurturing an ambition to end her own self-doubt. She now tutors others in the use of crystals to empower them to develop their own way in life. She lays a mixture of tiger's-eye, citrine, amethyst, labradorite, and rose quartz on clients while gently working on them in a form of spiritual coaching, using her hands to pull out bad energy.

"I'm just the channel to draw it out," she explains. "I see in my mind where to lay my hands to draw it out; it's a gift." Afterward, Knowles talks with her clients about color, recommending a crystal for them to work with on their own.

Knowles credits her state of calm to crystals, and in particular selenite, but the first crystal she fell in love with was a jagged-edge amethyst, at the young age of seven. From an early age she heard voices, which upset her

OPPOSITE Rock-crystal-
and-sapphire necklace by
Fabio Salini and a crystal
ring by Pebble London

because she didn't understand what they were or what to do with them, leading to feelings of isolation for a long time. "My sister would go out buying sweets, and I brought back rocks and crystals, because I instinctively found them comforting, like holding a teddy bear," she says.

During her twenties, crystals littered her bedroom floor, and Knowles kept them lined up on a ledge in the office between herself and the media group's CEO, who insisted on referring to her protective crystal barrier as "a wall of tat." It wasn't until her book, *The Power of Crystal Healing*, published a couple of years ago that she gained the confidence to quit her full-time job.

"I knew crystals worked because I'd spent so much time doing it," Knowles says. In her experience there are many "heavy bits" we keep buried that feed our self-doubt, and making long-lasting changes requires hard work. The most important requirement for this quest is patience. "Stones help everyone be less scared of letting go, and exploring in a nontraditional way how you can change," she asserts.

It's easy to blame situations or other people, but selenite can help you be accountable for what may be triggering self-doubt so that you can respond to it in new creative ways. Coco Chanel famously said, "Before you go out, look in the mirror and take one thing off." We need to drop a mode of behavior that doesn't suit us anymore to feel—and therefore look and act—our best.

The Window Stone

Selenite offered support to the Aztec people and their Toltec predecessors, who used the stone during full-moon rituals. Similarly, early sites in the American Southwest include ceremonial stone chambers called *kivas* that may have had narrow openings through which shafts of moonlight would enter only at the equinox or solstice. Basketry shields woven from fibrous plants have been discovered at the Mesa Verde archaeological site in Colorado; these were painted blue and green, with a rim of red, and sprinkled with powdered selenite, probably for spiritual sustenance.

One of the earliest known descriptions of selenite, below, comes from a text on herbal medicine, *De Materia Medica*, by Pedanius Dioscorides, an ancient Greek physician and botanist, who wrote it between 40 and 90 CE. The five volumes were translated into English in 1655.

> Lapis Selenites which some have called Aphroselenon because it is found in ye night-time, full in ye increase of ye moon. But it grows in Arabia, being white, transparent, light: filing it they give ye dust for a drink to ye epilepticall; but the women use it to hang it about them for an Amulet, & it is thought that being bound to trees, it makes them bear fruit.

Dioscorides also observed that at night, selenite would illuminate the place next to it because the gemstone was thought to contain the image of the moon inside. This could be because of the stone's pellucid effect channeling the changing image of the moon each day. Some descriptions make selenite sound similar to moonstone, though the two stones have vastly differing appearances and properties. Selenite was called *lunaris* in Latin, meaning "pertaining to the moon."

Pliny the Elder made lists of quarry sites where selenite was found, referring to it as *lapis specularis* (specular stone), which means "window stone." He described the ease with which it could be split into sheets as thin as required to admit light. Selenite is easily cut into thin sheets and has a hardness of only 2 on the Mohs scale, making it flexible enough to bend by hand, which is why it served as windowpanes up to as late as the seventeenth century.

In Roman times, the stone became highly fashionable. The rich were inspired to follow the lead of emperors Nero and Tiberius and install selenite windows in their villas. Not only were banqueting rooms, baths, and entire porticos secured against the weather in this way, but Pliny also described how it was used to protect apple trees and vines from wind and rain while allowing pure sun and daylight to enter freely. This sounds like an early version of the greenhouse that apparently allowed the table of Tiberius to be supplied with cucumbers throughout the year.

During the fifth century, the Roman Basilica of Santa Sabina was built using a new, simpler architectural style that would come to represent early Christian churches. Large thin sheets of selenite were fixed in the windows to spread light throughout the colonnaded nave.

> "You teach (though we learn not) a thinge unknowne
>
> To our late times, the use of specular stone,
>
> Through which all things within without were shown.
>
> Of such were temples; so, and if such you are Being and seeming is your equal care;
>
> And virtue's whole sum is but 'Know' and 'Dare.'"
>
> —JOHN DONNE, LETTER TO THE COUNTESS OF BEDFORD

Over time, interior designers, mindful of selenite's aesthetics, feel-better factor, and energy-directing qualities have elevated it from windowpanes into home decor for walls and floors. Selenite can be used in a functional manner in light fixtures, coffee tables, and objets d'art, with the stones raised on plinths like sculptures to energetically balance interiors. Wardrobes make another good spot for selenite, because it acts as a celestial vacuum cleaner, sucking up negativity and old stale energy from your clothes and belongings.

An added bonus is that ghosts or noncorporeal entities don't like to reside where selenite lives. No ghosts could possibly survive in the Hollywood Hills home of jewelry designer Robert Procop, who had twenty-four tons of selenite from Morocco, along with rock crystal from the Americas, trucked up as far as possible, and then hand carried into the house. It took three weeks. The stone is worked into two crystal fireplaces and a bar. Outside, the selenite shimmers against white walls, looking like tall translucent sandcastles with rock crystal- and rose quartz–pointed turrets. One bathroom is lined and decorated with spears and spikes of selenite, rock crystal, and rose quartz.

"Let's put it this way," Procop says. "I don't need to drink coffee when I wake up and walk into the bathroom in the morning." The leftover stone was transported to the home of actor Robert Downey Jr., where it was laid beneath and around his swimming pool.

Unhelpful thinking and behavior could be considered "ghosts" lingering from your childhood or other past events, subconsciously trapping you in unhelpful doubt. Any secrets or lies you or your family have been nurturing might need to be exorcised by selenite. Once you're aware of these "ghosts," you'll notice when they reappear. Then you can use selenite to adjust your reactions to them and direct your thoughts away from the subconscious seeds of doubt. Figure out who are the friendly ghosts, and strengthen your resolve against the harmful ones.

That includes other unwelcome phantoms. A friend places selenite by the windowsills and doorways of a room to keep it neutral and calm and stop her from vacuuming negative energy from others. It helps her feel more powerful when people come to her house. When necessary, crystal grids that include selenite can be strategically placed below floorboards or in ceilings to heal the home, improve the flow of energy, and support a calm atmosphere.

One friend had a crystal healer who'd studied ancient wisdom and the original patterns of temples lay stone grid floors in exact healing proportions, with a large "generator" crystal in a hollow space in a wall to amplify their energy.

ABOVE Erasing self-doubt with a selenite pillar at Bamford Haybarn

She was aiming to harmonize the space and block negative energy. When anger does arise in the home, the grid makes it easier for that energy to dissipate. And visitors feel the energy when they walk in, little realizing they are, in effect, walking over a crystal temple. Like many women who excel in their fields, my friend still has lurking feelings of self-doubt and thinks of the selenite as her floor armor, dispelling those feelings by surrounding her with a protective aura.

Exorcism & Optimism

Selenite has elements of both spiritual investment and art that is all about catching and reflecting light with its clear, shining white surfaces. Internally, selenite can help you review the progress you're making and clear confusion in a mind riddled with self-doubt. When we are criticized, it's easy to feel disappointment and slip into a doubting mood, but most comments aren't personal. What people say and how they react are motivated by their own thoughts about themselves, so try not to misinterpret them and build unnecessary self-doubt. Get a boost of optimism from your selenite while focusing on its lunarlike calm to view any setback as temporary. The work we undertake and any creative process can involve a struggle of confidence, and we ask ourselves, *What if people don't like what I've done?* The negative voice can be persuasive, but keep it at bay and don't let it hold you back.

Ancients believed selenite gave strength and a new energy to penetrate tired muscles. I believe this idea of renewed flexibility is actually the ability to perceive the successful steps you're taking every day. We don't all have the obviously fruitful careers of Gwyneth Paltrow or J. K. Rowling, but remember that celebrities' lives in reality are not as golden and effortless as they appear in the media.

Everyone battles with the demons of self-doubt at different stages. Each life has its own trials. It's never a smooth road, but the ability to bounce back from setbacks is crucial. Selenite gives you the clear vision to see those pitfalls and step around them. And even if you do fall in headfirst, selenite will help you scramble out and reevaluate. My friend at the start of this chapter, who went to Millbrook, swears she saw a selenite wand turn black at the tip when a healer placed it over her head as it pulled a dark energy from her body. Hold that thought when your sit with your selenite.

Last year I received a Christmas package from Brazil from jeweler Ara Vartanian. I unwrapped a cloudy piece of rock crystal large enough to sit upright in the palm of my hand. The festive period was taking its toll on me, and as I was headed to a crystal sound bath, I decided to take my new crystal with me. Apart from any other benefits, lying still for thirty minutes sounded tempting. The sound specialist began by harnessing the reverberating sounds and crystal vibrations in bowls of different shapes and sizes. I lay expectant on the floor as at first her baton in the bowl made barely a whisper. Soon it began to come in loud echoing waves as she used bigger bowls, and slowly I became immersed in sound that was vibrating through my chest so hard I barely noticed the selenite wands waving above me. I had been told this was a fast track to a meditative state of mind, and maybe it was given extra strength by the crystal I held tight. In any case, I left as recharged as if I'd had a power nap.

Later I reflected on the purity and simplicity of the technique. It felt like I had returned to a ritual one of my ancestors might have experienced. With the selenite, I felt as if we were tapping into the wisdom of ages through paraphernalia our forebears would have relied on to survive their difficult day-to-day lives. Although we might use stones as home and personal decor, we also value them as keepsakes and heirlooms from the past. Experiencing this age-old tradition created a feeling in me of sisterhood with the ancients. The goal of all research into natural history is to realize the full connection with human experience, including the humble triviality of man in comparison with the infinite power of nature.

The ancients personalized their surroundings and environment. Volcanoes, mountains, and lakes were both landmarks and the dwelling places of divine ancestors and spirits, making them sacred places. Ceremonies and rituals venerated the earth that sustained them and that released the precious material of crystal and stone. Use selenite to garner a sense of gratitude, which helps you keep the knocks of life, minor rejections, or rebuffs in perspective, seeing them as part of the great voyage of life.

It's important not to fall into the gloomy trap of social media designed to engender self-doubt and the unhealthy game of comparison to others—it's far better to compare yourself to *you*. Keep a journal or notes so you can jot down how far you've come and what obstacles you've overcome. It's important to celebrate your accomplishments and not be dejected by setbacks. Use the written evidence of the good to challenge negative thinking when it hovers over you.

Keep score of your selenite to check your progress. I'd suggest keeping a realistic record of the ways selenite has worked for you when you've felt overwhelmed. If you found selenite helpful in an attack of self-doubt, that's not only worth a high grade but it's also a powerful piece of information. Another time if it doesn't work so well, don't despair; cleanse the crystal and set it aside for a while until you're ready to try again. Remember that we're driven by stubborn subconscious beliefs. When they're limiting, we close ourselves off from opportunity, so keep waving them away with selenite and slowly the stone will help you install a new constructive vision of yourself. Keep hold of selenite and drop the doubts.

SOPHIE PENDLETON ——— Opening to Inspiration

It wasn't until jewelry designer Sophie Pendleton's divorce that she felt she needed crystals. She says her first crystal memories were of the agate and onyx jewels that swung around the neck of her artist mother when Sophie was growing up in Paris. As a teenager, she moved to California, where she studied business and psychology at Pepperdine University, and discovered turquoise at flea markets. A subsequent move to Asia, where she opened a children's gift boutique in Singapore, prompted her third distinct crystal memory: a crystal healing in Bali. She did it purely for the experience; she never thought she would need it. But everything changed when she separated from her husband.

That difficult time created a perfect storm of self-doubt that impacted every area of her life. One thing that helped her feel stronger was wearing rose-quartz and rock-crystal amulets inscribed with words such as *strength*, *faith*, and *harmony*. She believes the combination of the stones themselves with the words was particularly uplifting. She imagined them as a shield of protection around her.

She visited a reiki healer in Bali who advised her to connect with selenite, so she bought a few crystals to put on her desk and keep around the house. She also chose a simple pendant that she kept with her all the times.

"When I traveled and didn't have it with me, I noticed," she explains. "I felt like I needed to have it. I associated it with the healing session I'd received, which was very powerful, and by carrying the selenite I was taking a little piece of that with me. Stones are talismans when you're feeling vulnerable."

Did selenite and other crystals help her through the divorce? "Well," she stops and thinks for a moment, "actually, I think it helped me with more than that. It helps every day with inspiration and opened up something new inside me, which I hadn't been tapping into."

Some of Pendleton's selenite had to be shipped back from Singapore to her new London home. "I can't wait to get them back," she says. "They're very special, and I like to be surrounded by them. I do feel differently about the ones that gave me strength through the divorce. I have a gratitude for them."

When asked how she reconciles her crystals with her psychology studies, she responds, "A crystal jewel can have talismanic energy that makes a great companion in lonely or confused times. There's a power to the mind, and some people like to have a connection with something to feel more balanced."

BLACK

black tourmaline

Recharging and bolstering defenses to cope with social-media stress

COLOR SPECTRUM:
Licorice black, sometimes with flecks of silvery mica inside in vertically streaked prismatic crystals

FOUND: Sri Lanka; Brazil; Nepal; Africa; Pakistan; and California, Maine, New Hampshire, and New York in the United States

Ancient magicians are reported to have used black tourmaline when casting spells. In the age of 24/7 technology and social-media stress, we clearly need this stone's powers. Tourmaline is an ideal stone for our times because it provides protection against voices of hate, intolerance, and bigotry.

When we are overwhelmed by stress from electronic devices, black tourmaline can rapidly absorb negative energy and mental pollutants to balance disruptive energies. It can also provide psychic protection, strengthening your auric field like a great broom sweeping away the bad, and then replacing it with positive thoughts and actions.

Balance & Detachment

I remember when receiving an email was exciting. In 1998, these electronic messages were thrilling enough to support the premise of the movie *You've Got Mail* starring Tom Hanks and Meg Ryan. Things have changed. We now spend a large percentage of our time checking emails, texts, social media, and the myriad ways people now get hold of us both in and out of working hours. Increasingly, we live in an "always-on" culture, which can be unhealthy. Studies are showing that unconstrained social media can be detrimental to our mental health, leading to worry, anxiety, and depression.

There are plenty of upsides to all these means of communication—for instance, instant internet shopping or using FaceTime to keep in touch with absent friends or family—but no one is immune to the potential downsides of technology. Nothing beats face-to-face communication, as we need to hear the timbre of a voice and look into someone's eyes to fully understand their meaning. Quickly dashed-off texts are a minefield, highly prone to misinterpretation.

OPPOSITE My black tourmaline carried back from Los Angeles, resting on my iPhone alongside a rock crystal on my desk

Good communication is the key to every relationship. But now a new complaint has entered the lexicon: "excessive person-machine relationship." And given that our phones are always so close, as if they're tethered to our anatomy, I'd say it's pretty common issue.

———————

A couple of years ago, media personality Kendall Jenner came to terms with her relationship with technology. "I got robbed and I had my stalkers. That's why I don't really like going out anymore. That's why I don't tweet or Instagram. That gives me anxiety, too. I swear, it's the craziest thing," she said.

You don't have to be an A-lister to get palpitations looking at unread emails and texts, which tend to accumulate at a frightening speed. In my own case, I use my phone as an alarm clock, so I was sleeping with it nearby and could not turn it off completely—which meant I was waking up all the time. Now I switch to airplane mode and cover the phone with a black tourmaline, and I sleep much better.

Designer Victoria Beckham uses an entirely different method to allay anxiety during her fashion shows. "I'm a really positive thinker," she says. "I have no time for anything negative. I've bought crystals for all my team, so they carry them, too."

I brought back an opaque piece of black tourmaline from Los Angeles, which now sits beneath my computer. Glancing at the stone quickly, you might think I've left a piece of coal there. Does it dispel the electromagnetic field around my desk and cleanse my mind? I hope so. What I do know is that this is the computer where I feel inspired and comfortable to write.

Author and spiritual teacher Claudia Navone sleeps with a tourmaline at the base of her bed whenever she feels unsafe. The stone draws toxic emotions out through her feet, turning them into a powerful earth-healing energy. Another friend stashes one in the glove box of her car for protection on the road. It's good to sleep with one under your pillow, too, for a refreshing recharge; it subconsciously reminds you to dump leftover tribulations at the end of the day—it never helps to sleep on the negative.

For the holidays this year, I'm making oversize Christmas party-poppers wrapped around a joke, paper hat, and small pebbles of black tourmaline, because I know at some point in the day everyone will be on their mobile phones.

———————

During the Victorian and Edwardian periods, among the "fairer sex," black was a color reserved for mourning, servants, and office and shop employees. It didn't become fashionable until 1926, when *Vogue* featured on its cover a simple black dress in crêpe de Chine accessorized with a string of pearls and a cloche hat. *Vogue* described this dress as "The Ford," referring to the inexpensive, mass-produced Model T, which had originally been made only in black. In the context of the time, the name meant that the "little black dress" made "chic" available to women of all classes, the same way the Model T had democratized car ownership. *Vogue* predicted this dress would become a uniform, and women responded by nailing the new color to their masts and sailing onto the horizon wearing black. Iconic designer Coco Chanel later claimed, "I imposed black. It's still going strong today. It wipes out everything else around."

ABOVE Black tourmaline chunks collected inside weathered wooden bowls make a soothing room feature by Anna Unwin at Aubespoke Studio

When feeling under attack from an electrical overload, use black tourmaline. Keep the stone handy when scrolling through Instagram and other social media; some of it has a purpose, but both time and rationality can be abandoned as you dawdle over other people's lives. A precious hour spent feeding others' egos with "likes" so that they feel better about themselves could have been spent shaping a better morning for yourself.

Instagram is the parade ground where narcissists march. Narcissism is tagged as a fixation with oneself, one's appearance, or public persona, and it has always existed. A well-preserved fresco was recently uncovered in a bedroom at Pompeii depicting a story from Greek mythology. Narcissus was a hunter who fell in love with his own image reflected in a pool of water, and fearful of disturbing the water and his love disappearing, held his unwavering gaze until death.

We constantly rub up against vain, self-centered behavior on social media, though it's easy to be seduced by a narcissist's charm, grandiose schemes, or hollow claims of affection because we all want to fit in and belong. But it can quickly flip to the dark side, becoming demeaning and destructive. Black tourmaline can help you unpack the conflicting feelings around social media

and posts that evoke fear of missing out (FOMO). *You're my best friend! I love you!* and amusing hashtags about the night before are fun when you're one of the group. But when you're, as we say in London, NFI (Not F-ing Invited), anxiety can creep in.

Tourmaline builds a black barrier of protection to keep these unhelpful thoughts at bay mentally, and when you're in constant contact with other people's energies, it's particularly helpful worn as a ring or piece of jewelry. Black tourmaline helps neutralize the garbage we receive from people and devices. I know a nurse who always wears black tourmaline because she says at work in a hospital it's common to feel that her energy is absorbing the negative. She needs to dispel it, in much the same way that ancient magicians used it for protection when casting spells, in case their curses bounced back at them.

"We live in a funny time," says British businesswoman Carole Bamford, pointing at her mobile phone. "We're too reliant on this and it's creating a lot of anxiety." Bamford places a black tourmaline pyramid on her desk to make her feel protected. She found it on one of her travels foraging in the Indian markets of Jaipur. "The dustier and more obscure, the better," she admits, smiling. When she looks for stones, she's attracted by their shape and colors, using them to calm her mind, get in touch with her emotional instincts, and remind her to be grateful each day for the opportunities that come her way as well as break overreliance on technology.

Her desire has been to create holistic spaces that reflect her holistic values and encourage other women to be who they want to be and find their inner voices. With a series of workshops, organic and sustainable products, and crystal sessions, her brand teaches how to abandon the self-doubt social media can provoke and to live more joyfully. There are baskets of black tourmaline, rock crystal, amethyst, and fluorite stones and heart-shaped rose quartz and rock crystal in the Bamford stores. "People are constantly picking them up because we're all searching for something missing from our lives," she says. By her bed, she keep rose quartz, with holy water from Lourdes, which she infuses with holy basil and medicinal herbs to create what she calls her own "moon water." The rose-quartz love is balanced with black tourmaline. "I feel better having black tourmaline all around at the moment," she explains, "because it reminds me I don't have to get so emotionally involved."

The Ash Puller

Tourmaline isn't only found in black; it also presents in rainbow shades—although the two weren't recognized as the same stone until quite late. In green, tourmaline is often referred to as "Brazilian emerald." Blue is called indicolite. Red, violet, or pink shades are termed rubellite. A remarkable green-and-pink variety from Brazil looks like a miniature watermelon; the green on the outside fades to a strong pink inside—nothing is lacking but the seeds. The Egyptians believed that tourmalines got their colors when they broke through a rainbow while pushing their way up out of the earth.

OPPOSITE Black slices of agate designed into a belt by Peter Adler and worn with a long quartz pendant by Harris Zhu

The earliest written mention of black tourmaline comes from about 1400 CE, when it was described as *Schorl*; possibly the name was derived from the German village Zschorlau, in Saxony, where deposits of black stone were found in an old tin mine. Later, the more brilliantly colored stones were discovered in Sri Lanka (then Dutch Ceylon) and brought to Europe in great quantities during the eighteenth century by the Dutch East India Company. Beginning in the sixteenth century, it became known as tourmaline, thought to have been derived from the Sinhalese word *toramalli*, which translates as "something small from the earth" or "mixed gems."

A story is told about a warm summer's day in Amsterdam when a group of children playing in a courtyard with a few stones brought back from Sri Lanka noticed how they came to life on the hot paving stones, attracting a nearby pile of dust and ashes lying in the street. This magnetic power to attract (and to repel) powdery dust particles and straw led to the stones being called, in Dutch, *aschentreckers*—ash-pullers. Early Dutch traders began to use tourmalines to clean ash from their pipes, and elsewhere they were referred to as the "Ceylonese magnet."

When tourmaline is heated, it has the ability to produce negative and positive charges at either end, like a battery. This property is termed *pyroelectricity*. The stone also exhibits piezoelectricity when it is rubbed vigorously or put under stress. As a result, tourmalines have been used in thermometers and depth and pressure gauges, and more recently for electrical tuning circuits, as high frequencies can be passed through the stone with no detrimental effect. This attribute could be one of the reasons that tourmaline provides a wonderful sense of balance and helps you become less emotionally involved in charged issues.

Many practitioners highlight the dangers of electromagnetic stress and Wi-Fi, which they believe can create imbalances that damage our health. Tina Cutler, who works in London and Ibiza in Spain, surrounds her phones and computers with black tourmaline and shungite to protect herself from electromagnetic fields as well as the negativity she's clearing from clients, which tends to stick around. "I like to keep my house as clean as possible," she tells me. (By *clean*, read "clear of bad vibes.") "Sometimes I can feel drained, so I often put the stone in my bath. The skin's the biggest organ, so I think it's the best way to absorb its qualities."

When you're playing games via social media, imagine the particles of negativity being sucked into the opaque center of your stone in the same way that Dutch children and traders drew ash with theirs. Your tourmaline pebbles will act as a lustrous buffer against the mental exhaustion and ensuing feelings of unworthiness FOMO can leave. It's quite satisfying when

1 Black tourmaline egg

2 Black-and-white fossilized agate

3 Necklace of black agate slices

4 Pink-and-black agate bowl

5 Smoky-quartz and labradorite pebbles

you wash the stone to visualize any disappointing drivel being flushed away like waste. And as social media can be a top time-waster, the tourmaline will prompt you to not let your valuable time be disposed of along with that waste.

On a positive note, holding your tourmaline at the end of the day when you're tired can be like taking an imaginary bath, helping you unwind as you symbolically soak away particles of dirt you've attracted during the day. Then again, you could take an actual bath, switch off your phone and leave it somewhere where you can't see it, and place your black tourmaline in the soap dish.

American mineral collector George Kunz effectively altered early-twentieth-century conceptions of "precious" when he popularized tourmalines as jewelry. Until the 1920s, the only stones considered precious were the big four: sapphire, emerald, ruby, and diamond. Kunz took advantage of his close proximity to the stones buried all across the United States while on voyages of discovery to North Carolina, California, Montana, and Utah.

New York City had been rapidly expanding since the late nineteenth century, and with so many excavations for new roads, tunnels, and railroads always underway, the underlying bedrock was continually exposed. One railroad excavation between 171st Street and Fort Washington in Washington Heights threw up a nine-inch-long black tourmaline embedded in gray quartz. Kunz delighted in these discarded by-products of digging, and by the age of twenty he had amassed four hundred gems and precious stones, which he sold to the University of Minnesota.

"A mineralogist collects everything that nature produces, and those with least commercial value often have the greatest value in his eyes," he said of his lifelong gemstone quest. One of his discoveries, a powder-pink stone, was named *kunzite* in his honor. Another discovery was a particularly distinctive tourmaline from Mount Mica in Maine. In 1876, he persuaded Charles Tiffany, who'd recently founded his eponymous store, to purchase it. In 1927, Kunz was interviewed about the experience in an article for the *Saturday Evening Post:*

> So one day, buckled in youth, I wrapped a tourmaline in a bit of gem paper, swung on a horse car, and all the way to my destination rehearsed my arguments. Arrived there, I was finally received by the managing head of what was even then the largest jewelry establishment in the world, and showed him my drop of green light.

A few short years after that sale, Kunz became the resident gem expert at Tiffany, collecting stones for some of the great names of that period—including a research collection for inventor Thomas Edison and the famous J. P. Morgan–Tiffany gem collection at the American Museum of Natural History.

Mount Mica, where Kunz had found his brilliant green tourmaline, formed part of the rugged Streaked Mountain range. The area held remarkable tourmaline deposits that were first discovered by two students. Augustus Choate Hamlin described the discovery in his book *The Tourmaline*, published in 1873:

> It was on the last day of autumn; and the glimmering rays of the setting sun were gilding with renewed splendor the faded colors of the landscape as the students were passing over the top of one of the lowest knolls. The view of the distant mountains, the intervening valleys softened with purple shadows, the patches of green grass in the meadows untouched by early frost, the variegated hues of the forest leaves left by the autumnal winds, the broad extents of russet brown of the stubble fields, contrasting vividly with the glorious hues of the sunset sky, composed a scene of exquisite loveliness.

The youths lingered on the hilltop to view the panorama until the valleys were veiled in shadows as dusk approached. Otherwise, they might never have seen the vivid green crystal glinting in the twilight on the root of an upturned tree. They took the crystal and decided to return at daybreak to continue their search for others, but overnight the hill was covered in thick snow, and it remained so until spring. Once the snow melted, a treasure of black, green, red, and yellow crystals was uncovered, deposited in a ledge perforated with a honeycomb of cavities where decomposing rock was crumbling away to expose the stones. The fame of Mount Mica spread, and over a period of forty years the finest gems and specimens of tourmaline were produced from mines there and in California. In 1912, newer and larger deposits were found in Brazil and Afghanistan.

Clarity & Perspective

I bought my black tourmaline in California because Azalea Lee, who conducts seminars, readings, and crystal workshops in Los Angeles, told me that everyone should have one. "It's a staple crystal," she explains, "I don't know a person who doesn't need it." A former Hollywood costume designer, Lee is part of the new wave of entrepreneurs lending a sophisticated aesthetic to the domain of alternative healing. Her white-walled gallery-style showroom boasts display cases of carefully curated natural art objects. There, Lee teaches people how to interpret crystals and make the ephemeral into something more tangible.

During my crystal reading, Lee took me on a two-hour guided journey, searching for internal blockages that she aimed to clear. Whether it is an old memory or a significant moment, tourmaline can help you analyze it and see it from a different point of view. Tourmaline is important during this exercise because, Lee says, "It turns the negative into positive. Basically, it takes the shit from our lives and makes it into compost."

How many times do you use the word *stress* in a week? It seems to be endemic in work and home lives, and now *technostress* adds a whole new realm to the term. Technostress encompasses a range of behaviors and feelings of addiction around our devices, varying from overuse to FOMO to its dimension as an additional "job" added to our workday. Fortunately, black tourmaline can counter this tension, excessive worry, and obsessive behavior.

Lee wears a river-tumbled black tourmaline ring when she's writing emails. "It acts like my shield, keeping the negative away," she says. These stones "are a workhorse; use them to do the heavy lifting." But they don't offer a quick fix. Lee emphasizes that we should work with tourmaline for the rest of our lives, in a "deep and personal relationship."

Clever algorithms have been devised for electronic devices to tempt us to the dark side, but the jet black of tourmaline can pull us back from the edge of the techno-abyss. Parents of teenagers have a particularly hard task before them in managing the effects of social media on young minds. The talk of bullying, drugs, and predators that takes place often on secret texting apps and chat forums is hard to monitor, especially when new comment sections and forums seem to spring up from nowhere.

I recently went to hear British American author, motivational speaker, and leadership guru Simon Sinek when he spoke in London recently on how digital addictions and cell phones impact relationships and ruin lives. A phone ping, he says, acts as a hit of dopamine to the brain, an instant spark we seek again and again. Having our devices constantly at hand means we're never truly alone, and this prevents young people from developing healthy coping strategies. Possibly we need to throw amethyst at this issue, as well as affix black tourmaline to the back of our phones.

Black tourmaline is something solid to rely on in the midst of this ambiguous, ubiquitous, hard-to-tackle issue. Electromagnetic radiation increasingly engulfs the space around us. People complain about clusters of white dots in front of their eyes at the end of a long phone call or buzzing in their ears. Some medical practitioners believe that, although we don't know the results yet, fallout from devices is hurtling toward us.

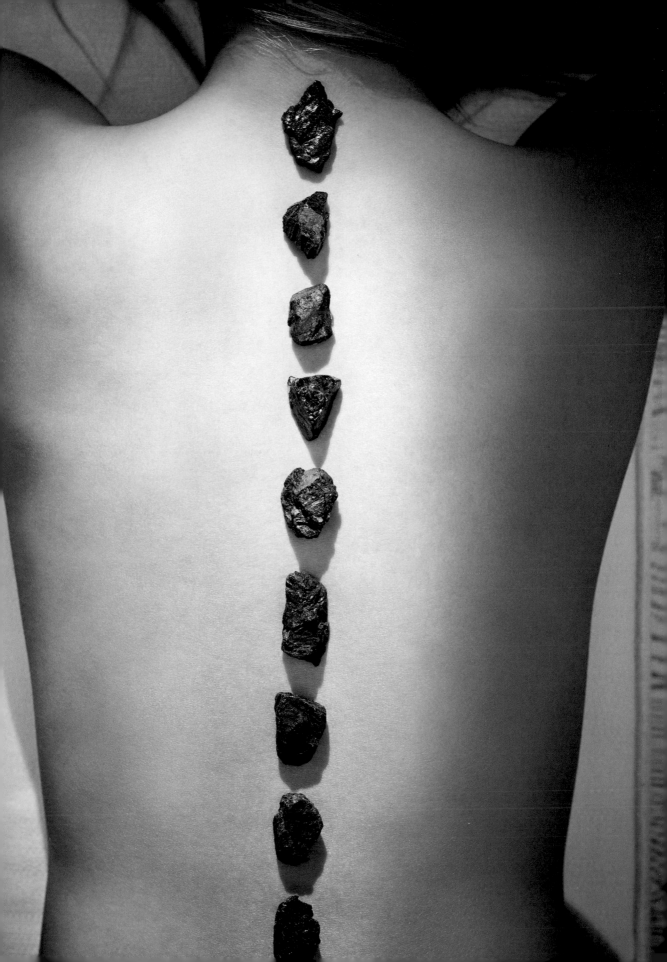

Keeping up with social media can make you feel out of control; the antidote is to let black tourmaline draw the negative out, and in the act of letting go, you can regain control of your mental health. Black tourmaline can help you detox from your digital intake. It's certainly to be encouraged for anyone who's particularly sensitive—those who are prone to internalize criticism and other's opinions—and who may need guarding against those who are more forceful.

Think of tourmaline as an effective bouncer, ready to chuck out anything you haven't invited into your environment. Although no ray of light can struggle through the blackness, paradoxically, this absence of color can produce light in your life, which contributes to a sense of solidity and comforting steadfastness.

KATIE SPICER ———— Powering Down Social-Media Stress

In spite of the benefits of tech empowerment, young New Yorker Katie Spicer became a self-confessed slave to technology with an acute case of FOMO. Her decluttering business was organized online, and technology met all her shopping requirements and dominated her social life and relationships, even delivering her boyfriend from a dating website.

"I kept comparing various aspects of my life with my friends on social media," she says. "I began to feel I was missing out, or that there might be better options for me out there and that I was getting things wrong."

Spicer was following Instagram feeds of a few supermodels and realized it was making her feel pressured into trying to conform to a one-dimensional physical ideal guaranteed to make her feel she'd failed. She was aware of the hazards of twenty-four-hour connectivity to self-esteem—she'd seen the experience of a few college friends who were cyber-shamed—but nonetheless she fully integrated her devices into her social and emotional life.

"The first thing I'd do in the morning is look at Twitter or Instagram gossip," she says. "When I had a new business and should have been getting up and starting my day working, I was time-wasting on things that I didn't like about myself."

One night, when she rolled over in bed to check the Insta-judgments underneath her feed at 2 a.m., she realized that her relationship with technology was unhealthy. "I knew I needed to break my intense relationships with devices," she explains. "I decided to go cold turkey, but I knew I needed some help."

She placed several chunks of black tourmaline around her home and office, and every night put her mobile phone in airplane mode and covered it with tourmaline to reduce the radiation. She also attached a small piece of the stone to the back of the cover during the day. She cleansed her feed so that she stopped scrolling through things that triggered her anxiety, and began ignoring the nagging notifications. "I'm more careful how I use technology now, and keep black tourmaline to protect me from trawling through social media as well as from the bad vibes," she says.

It's made Spicer feel that she has more time, and she doesn't feel pulled in a hundred different directions at once. Black tourmaline has freed her from the technostress of her machines.

GOLD

pyrite

Building vitality and productivity to realize your potential

COLOR SPECTRUM: Metallic gold clusters of small geometric crystals in cubic and dodecahedral shapes and clustered pebbles

FOUND: Italy; China; Peru; Spain; Australia; and Nevada, Arizona, Pennsylvania, Illinois, Vermont, Minnesota, Wisconsin, Montana, and Missouri in the United States

When we're young, the world is full of possibilities, and we believe we can be whatever we want. After we reach adulthood, our time is spent being pulled in a hundred directions, and our carefree approach to life becomes tainted with fear. What if we never fulfill our potential? In the quiet of the night, it is easy to be swept away by thoughts of what we could have been and are not. Dissatisfaction about our lives or achievements can creep upon us unexpectedly.

Time management might be the most valuable skill women possess right now, because we need and want to do so much more than previous generations. The pressure increases as we strive to be women who can do everything. I remember a particularly poignant meeting one day in the *Vogue* boardroom when a successful forty-two-year-old designer told me her recent round of in-vitro fertilization had failed. "I was told we could have it all, so I built my business and waited to get pregnant," she explained sadly. "Now it looks like I won't be able to have a child, and I always saw myself as a mother."

As fast as we row our boat in one direction, the current changes and the mysterious flow of life pulls us to another destination entirely. We raise the pressure on ourselves because we're so fearful we won't reach our target of being the person we wanted to become. But who is that person, and how do we know when we've reached the goal? No one can ever tell you because there's no definitive answer—it's a whisper within yourself that only you can decipher. Hence the midlife cry, *What am I doing here?*

After reflecting on your life, you may feel that you didn't accomplish anything significant or make a difference. This can lead people to question their very existence, and the danger of that is that the achievements and securities we've painstakingly built begin to sway and waver in the midst of this existential downpour of soul-searching.

OPPOSITE My pyrite formation inside Plexiglas by Diane Kordas with smoky-quartz earrings and gold-flecked glass

Focus & Pragmatism

The antidote for such middle-of-the-night existential doubt is pyrite. This brassy yellow crystal can help you reach your potential—which is not the same as making it to the top or gaining riches. Rather, it is making steps toward an inner sense of joy and fulfillment that your life reflects your choices and priorities. With pyrite you can sensibly reevaluate to improve or change the things that aren't right for you. Realizations might dawn as you reflect on how lucky you've been and how pointless the activity of idly wishing for another life can be. This life is the one you have. It's yours to make the most of, and nurturing a perennial sense of disappointment is a fool's errand.

The night before I began to write this chapter, I piled my notes and research in front of the computer before going out to a dinner hosted by American designer Diane Kordas. I was seated next to British Iranian journalist Christiane Amanpour, the host of CNN's international interview program, and the rest of the table was equally stellar.

At one point in the evening, our hostess asked us to take turns around the table saying what we'd like the new year to deliver. "Consensus," answered Amanpour immediately, and actors Minnie Driver and Dougray Scott discussed the merits of being in the next Martin Scorsese movie. When my turn came, I blurted out, "Finish my crystal book." Immediately I felt self-conscious; in the midst of this high-achieving crowd, didn't I have a more worthy or loftier-sounding ambition? Why couldn't I say something more impressive— particularly in front of the admirable Amanpour, who is committed to using her voice to make the world a better place? Mine appeared like a fuzzy objective in direct contrast to her confident vision of global affairs. All of a sudden, my book felt so dinky, so small-fry.

At the end of the evening, Kordas handed out gifts. She had chosen a crystal to suit each of us. Actress Claire Forlani opened a small geode suspended in acrylic. In a moment of strange synchronicity, which happens around crystals, I unwrapped a gleaming pyrite. Kordas had no idea about the contents of my book or this chapter on pyrite that I would begin the following morning. What were the odds that, out of thirty or so crystals, she gave me the pyrite? And at the precise moment I doubted the book would fulfill its potential, she handed me pyrite on a plate.

The stone is suspended, so I can see the crystal in the round. Sitting on top of my desk, its yellow luster draws my eye as a reminder and to spark ideas, because it's a good stone for creative energy. When I look around, instead of seeing what I have achieved, like many of us I tend to focus on what I have not. We chastise ourselves with a deluge of "not good enough" thoughts that sweep us off course. The book is important to *me*, and that's all that matters. Most of our day-to-day achievements don't have a high profile nor do they hit prime-time television. Instead, they're small, but similar to the stacked golden cubes sitting in front of me, each one builds a block of self-belief on top of the one before, building to a sense of success.

These mesmerizing minerals are formed in cubic and stalactite-like forms that have a hardness of 6 to 6.5 on the Mohs scale. Their metallic gold color is that of riches, bound up for three thousand years with notions of idolatry, worldly power, and material wealth. The Egyptians believed that gold was the flesh of the gods; the pharaohs expressed their authority and closeness to the divine by bedecking their temples in gold. The hieroglyph for gold, *nub*, appears often; it looks like a necklace with pendant beads.

The history of gold has been linked to wealth and greed ever since Julius Caesar first minted gold coins as currency, and the mythical King Midas perished after his vain prayer for the golden touch. It also symbolizes immortality, because gold never tarnishes or corrodes. Pliny the Elder illustrated his disapproval for the pursuit of gold by writing:

> We probe her [Mother Earth's] entrails, digging into veins of gold and silver . . . we drag out her entrails . . . to be worn upon a finger.

All that glitters is not gold, however. Pyrite's gleam is not associated with hard cash and avarice but with accomplishment—work well done—in whatever particular form suits you. Pyrite balances the idea that you need to reach for what you want while also promoting the willingness to help others. How many times have you metaphorically kicked yourself for a lost opportunity when you haven't said what you want or think you deserve because of nerves, or fear of looking ridiculous, or simply of someone saying no to you? Pyrite will push you to ask for what you know you want without fear, because if you don't ask, you won't get.

Pyrite has an additional reputation as something of a trickster, entrapping the ignorant and blindly greedy. For centuries, many have believed they struck gold, only to find that in reality they had found pyrite, or fool's gold as it came to be known. (Completing the shimmering trail of look-alikes is marcasite, which has a paler shade and has often been confused for pyrite.)

ABOVE Rock crystal, pyrite, black tourmaline, and smoky quartz on the shelves of designer Ara Vartanian, overlooking Sao Paolo

Early European explorers came to the New World expressly to find gold, which Christopher Columbus had observed the natives wearing on his first voyage to the Americas: "Oh, most excellent gold! Who has gold has a treasure that even helps souls to paradise."

The government of Queen Elizabeth I encouraged groups of merchant adventurers to travel to the Americas. Literally tons of glittering metal were shipped back to Europe from these voyages to be sold to raise funds for further expeditions, as well as lure more immigrants to the colonies with the promise of riches.

Christopher Newport was captain of the *Susan Constant* in 1607, which carried male settlers to found Jamestown, Virginia, the first successful English settlement in North America. Newport shipped 1,100 tons of pale golden ore found near the settlement back to London for assay. Sadly, he was informed the cargo was pyrite.

Ignition & Support

Pyrite's name comes from the Greek *pyr*, meaning "fire." Striking a piece of this stone against a piece of flint produces sparks hot enough to ignite dried twigs. This made fire portable, which argues that pyrite played a fundamental part in the evolution of human civilization, as fire was vital for survival. Pyrite has been found in burial sites, leading to the assumption that a fire was believed to be needed in the afterlife.

In Greek mythology, hero Prometheus was credited with defying the gods by stealing fire and giving it to humanity, and came to represent the idea of striving to improve human existence. Without fire there could be no progress. Borrow the spark of pyrite to ignite your inner drive and advance; with Prometheus in mind, remember that your move forward can also enable the progress of those around you.

During the sixteenth and seventeenth centuries, the sparking ability of pyrite was used as a source of ignition in early firearms: a spring-driven serrated wheel rotated against a piece of pyrite. Think of the stone as igniting action within you, encouraging dynamism and confidence. No more hiding your light behind a bushel or inside a self-conscious shell.

This fiery energy of pyrite can ignite flames of confidence and action inside you, helping you identify your particular strengths and weaknesses and how to use them to your advantage. Success can come in any shape or size, and you need to pursue the course that reflects who you are and what will fulfill you. That won't necessarily be what people expect of you—or what you

ABOVE Pyrite spheres contrasting with the terminated points of rock-crystal spears, resting on a fossilized wood table

might have imagined for yourself when you were younger. The effort will certainly require honesty and authenticity.

Use pyrite in the office as a powerhouse of productivity. Place it near a task you've been delaying or procrastinating over that you know needs to be done. I use mine as a golden paperweight. It not only keeps my pile of research papers in check but prevents my mind from drifting and worrying about the work I haven't completed.

It helps to hold a golden cluster of pyrite in each hand when you need a refreshing burst of energy. In spite of its nickname, this stone can have a greater merit than gold. By reinforcing your version of success, it can encourage you to come out of your shell and have faith in your dynamism and confidence, which is invaluable.

Ironically, much of the gold mined today is found in the form of microscopic blebs, thin-walled airspaces trapped inside minerals, and pyrite ores are the richest source. Who's the fool now? Even if you didn't shine the brightest at school, that's no reason to hold yourself back. You can mine your hidden golden talents and become a life force in the present.

Pyrite flecks of golden mirrors shine in egg-shaped contemporary artworks by Amaryllis Fraser that look as if they've survived from antiquity. "I have a light obsession with pyrite, which is the stone of action. I love working with it— it attracts abundance and throws back what you want," Fraser says.

A few years ago, she was sitting on a train when a vision of a large crystal sculpture came into her head. Although she comes from an artistic family, Fraser had never painted or sculpted before. Shortly after, she began cutting pyrite, amethyst, and black tourmaline into chunky pieces and positioning them together like a jigsaw puzzle to match her vision, eventually fixing them onto a birch panel that hangs on a wall. They look like floating moons with a jagged lunar landscape of crystal. "I feel so different working with them," she says. "I'm elated with so much energy I feel like I've drunk fifty espressos—in a good way."

Fraser says she never knows exactly why she's drawn to different stones: "They're inanimate objects, but they hold emotions. Everyone goes through various stages of life. For instance, when you start to have a family you definitely get drawn to different stones."

She allows her two young children to choose the rock crystals they have in their bedrooms, and she has widened her artwork to include brass centerpieces for tables inlaid with pyrite and white quartz, and large coffee tables with acrylic tops filled with Herkimer diamonds and other quartz crystals. In her open-plan sitting room, two vast citrines rest on the floor in preparation for a new work, and fixed along the wall is a black tourmaline work with a pyrite heart beating through its gilded center.

Not only does pyrite feature in her work, it also inspires. "Pyrite is a stone for helping creative ideas be more active in the mind, and it gives you a sense of focus and concentration," she explains. In her work she also aims to connect others to pyrite's abundance. When we met, Fraser was working on a pure-white interactive crystal sculpture. On its side are symbols engraved in brass; the idea is to pick a daily crystal, which has a corresponding angel card describing its purpose.

1 Golden pyrite pendant

2 Natural pyrite formation

3 Pyrite heart

4 Silver pebbles

5 Rock-crystal cave

Scientists believe pyrite has been a key component of the earth's living systems throughout time—small crystals of it have been found in the cell walls of fossilized single-cell organisms that are 3.5 billion years old. Compositions of pyrite are used to investigate the earth's environment in the past and its evolution. These pieces of information about the surface environment of the planet can be used to help predict future changes. In *Pyrite: A Natural History of Fool's Gold*, geochemist David Rickard writes:

> We currently view the history of the Earth, understand much of its present workings and predict what will happen to our future environment through the prisms of tiny pyrite grains . . . These pyrite grains, which are spread throughout the Earth in time and space preserve much of the evidence of the nature of earlier Earths, as well as the balances and imbalances of our present system.

As greenhouse gas levels reach record heights, prompting the United Nations weather agency to warn that the window of opportunity to prevent catastrophic climate change has "almost closed," it's clear our civilization needs to activate a stronger connection with the earth. Pyrite helps you take action to support other human beings as well as the earth, and the courage to be assertive in your action. Pyrite's fire will ignite energy and spark the leader in you to take charge of larger tasks, as well as spur you to recycle, reject disposable plastic, and clear litter. Like pyrite crystals, these efforts build atop of each other to construct something of substance.

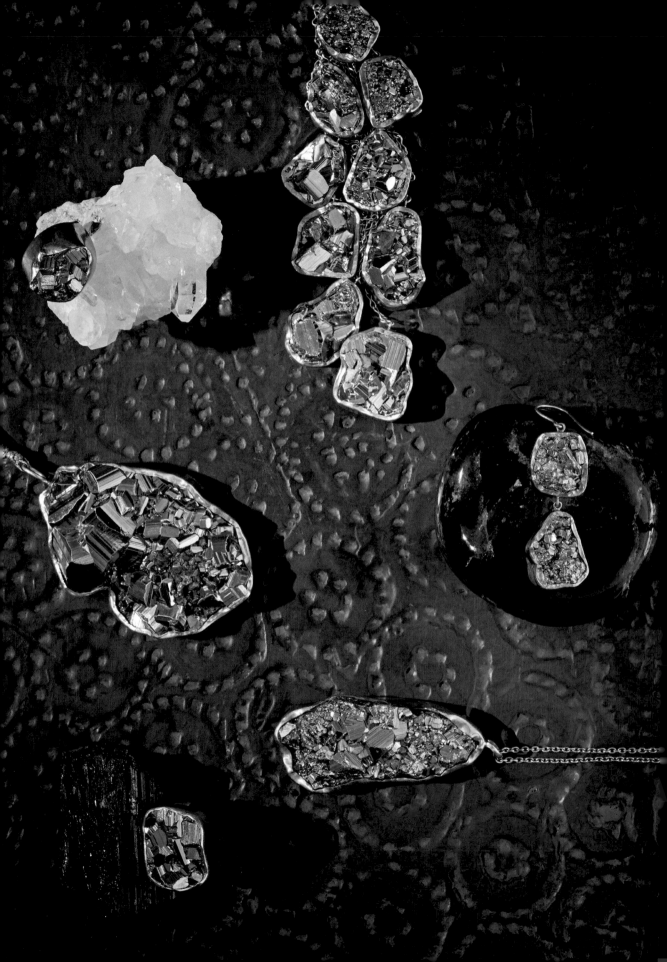

Building Blocks

For a few days each year, under the big skies shifting over the desert, Tucson, Arizona, plays host to rock hounds, New Agers, and stone dealers at the Gem, Mineral & Fossil Showcase. The city center becomes a fantastical place brimming with natural design in rock-crystal pillars, including amethyst caves so large your fingers get icy the farther inside you venture.

Away from the center of the gem show, where brown adobe-style buildings blend into the buff-colored sandy soil, is the spiritual home of the metaphysical brigade seeking an endorphin dump from rough-hewn pieces. Colorful pebbles, clusters of pyrite, and assorted rocks in small boxes can be bought for a few dollars from the back of a pickup truck or a motel bedroom. Trunks of petrified wood are brought in through rock-strewn acres of cacti and scrub to be shown in tents and pueblos alongside meteorites dropped from outer space and fossilized dinosaur bones, squid, ammonites, and the odd piece of "dino poop."

All around I can see sparkling rocks and geodes from American artisanal mines, such as Montana sapphires and fire agate, rutilated quartz from Brazil, and egg-size carats of gemstones. One pyrite I spotted, about a foot high, consisted of five large perfect cuboid blocks set at an angle atop of one another. The extraordinary formation was set onto a plinth and lit like a Modigliani sculpture. A stone statue doesn't need to be huge to make a significant impact; the pyrite's natural formation was as captivating as anything displayed in an art gallery.

Another way to employ the power of pyrite is to make a list of all the positive things about yourself, turn the list faceup, and place a pyrite on top; it will help you begin accepting that they are a vital part of you. As a result, your self-esteem will improve, which is what you need to activate any potential-fulfilling missions.

Pyrite is an excellent stone for helping students (and the rest of us) increase their focus and see things through to completion. Relationships, lack of hours in the day, exhaustion, and other excuses are cited as reasons not to continue with something, but more often than not these are a defense mechanism or shield to mask the secret inner panic that we may never accomplish our goals. This is when you most need pyrite to remind you that every step takes you to the next stage. Slowly, using pyrite, you learn to be a success.

OPPOSITE Pyrite jewels by Pippa Small on black tourmaline and rock crystal

When you hold a pyrite, hang on to your ideas of manifesting goals. Pyrite can train the muscle of resiliency, helping you acquire a can-do attitude and the courage to reach for your desires.

Fear of underachieving can hit at any age, but it's perhaps particularly stressful for the young. Recently, twenty-five-year-old model, entrepreneur, and social activist Leomie Anderson wrote on her retail platform's blog, "Why do I feel I'm running out of time to achieve my goals?" Reality was falling short of her expectations. "Every day I feel anxious," she continued.

There's a pleasing realization that comes with maturity that you're okay with not doing it all, or okay with not doing everything at the same time. It's important not to set your expectations too high. Sometimes fixating on chasing one goal, such as a career milestone, can close you off to other life opportunities. Pyrite may require you to concentrate on one goal at a time—building blocks again—while aiming for multifaceted satisfaction in all areas. However, the last thing you want to do is spend an entire lifetime polishing a dream while avoiding the risks that could enable it to happen and make you the happiest. Dreaming of changing your life—but not daring to do it—leads to a stagnancy of the soul, which undercuts life's pleasures. Like pyrite, there's a golden winner within you, and when you tap into it, your outer patina will reflect the sparkle.

Using the stone, you'll be better placed to take the following advice.

"Twenty years from now you will be more disappointed by the things you didn't do than by the things you did do. So throw off the bowlines, sail away from the safe harbor. Catch the trade winds in your sails. Explore. Dream. Discover."

—H. JACKSON BROWN JR., *P.S. I LOVE YOU*

We never know for sure what lies on the other side of a hill we need to climb or around a blind corner, but it would be boring to know exactly where life is taking us. Your potential lies just on the horizon; visualize it with pyrite, set your compass, and follow the gold-bricked road to the fulfillment of your dreams.

SUSAN FOSTER ——— Reaching for New Purpose

A few years ago, New York–based designer Susan Foster added pyrite to her collection of crystals. "It's about success, and I feel quite different when I use it in comparison to other stones," she says. With pyrite, she's found the courage to begin a charity for children that she'd been mulling over for some years.

Foster's Upper East Side apartment is dotted with stones; a large piece of quartz rests on her desk. "I chose it because it's so heavily included with rainbow clouds and feathers," she says. "It refracts rainbows all around my apartment." Another milky-quartz prism is placed on her nightstand.

"I lived in LA for twenty years, and that's the land of this type of metaphysics," she says. Foster explains that she feels something akin to a vibration going through her hands when holding crystals. It's very subtle, and you have to relax to feel it, which makes her believe there's a validity and purpose behind each crystal. "Enlightenment or protection?" she questions. "I don't know if any of that's true, but when I sit and meditate and hold one, I do feel better. Plants have a purpose in medicine, so I think crystals do too." Her go-to meditative companions are rock crystal and rose quartz, as well as, more recently, pyrite. "It's very centering," she tells me.

It was New York shaman and healer Deborah Hanekamp who suggested pyrite to Foster and gave her the "homework" of speaking certain words when immersed in a prescriptive bath of oatmeal, lavender, and rose oil, which began to shift her energy. Foster then became a global ambassador for the international children's charity World Vision, providing support to refugee camps in Syria, Lebanon, and northern Uganda.

Foster has harbored a lifelong ambition to inspire children with creativity. Recently, she launched a nonprofit art-therapy foundation called A Place to Be(ad) Me. Participants are New York children who've suffered domestic trauma; the foundation creates a safe haven for them. The children learn a range of skills from jewelry making to communication with the goal of helping them develop a sense of freedom, increased esteem, and recognition of their worth through creative outlets.

This idea of success is typical of pyrite: pursuing an accomplishment with the added benefit of desiring to pass it on to others. Pyrite provides a courage alert, a subtle reminder for Foster that change can be life-affirming for her as well as the young children her charity reaches. And in doing that, she doesn't merely tick a goal box, she realizes her dream.

Conclusion

If you remain undecided about which crystal to choose, you could take a look at one of the great repositories of minerals and crystals in public museums; an estimated five million have been gathered and preserved around the world. I've concentrated these chapters on the group of stones I think you should consider first to assist in contemporary life. These stones also have a history with the ancients, but you will find new "contemporary classics" in these collections, as they have been mined in the last few decades. The aesthetic appreciation of your crystal requires no scientific knowledge; it's all based on visual appeal. But I thought I'd end my research for this book back where I began, at London's Natural History Museum, with someone who does understand the complex system of atomic relationships, the consequence of the laws of physics and chemistry, and the geological and historical conditions required to form crystals.

The age of a stone is irrelevant for our purposes; and surprisingly, we have that in common with Mike Rumsey, who is the museum's senior curator of mineralogy. "We might have the geological understanding of how a volcano erupted, but we have a problem aging stones," he says. In spite of Rumsey's academic title, international acclaim, and deep understanding of the systemic mineralogical nomenclature focusing on unusual mineral phases, he is wearing jeans and his hair scraped back into a ponytail, just like the young rock hounds I saw at the Tucson gem fair.

"Often we can't date minerals unless they contain elements such as certain basalts, which we can date," he says. "But age is less important for mineralogists than it would be for paleontologists, who want to know where things fit in. Stones are forming and unforming all around us very slowly on a human scale."

If a Brazilian apatite were to arrive for Rumsey to assess, he'd be able to record where and how the stone was formed, but when it was created often remains speculation. Small stones can take as long as larger crystals to form—no one really knows. And contrary to the thought that woolly mammoths might have been roaming the earth above your crystal when it was formed, many examples are thought to be only ten thousand years old.

OPPOSITE Crystal-and-colored glass hanging mobile by Julia Condon in the home of Allegra Hicks

"Nature is diverse and complicated. There are so many variables. There's a lot we don't know and a huge amount of research to be done," he explains with excitement.

A range of minerals named after animals are displayed in cabinets at the museum. Trout stone from lower Austria has a texture recalling the fish scales of a brown trout. The spotted plumage of the European starling is visible in an agate called starling stone, and others have patterns comparable to animal skins. Tiger's-eye, leopard-skin-jasper, and zebra stone are placed together, along with hawk's-eye and cat's-eye winking with their optical effects. These 120,000 or so minerals and crystals in the museum have been amassed principally as scientific aids to help researchers gain a better understanding of the evolution of the planet, with the secondary artistic value of inspiring people. Does Rumsey ever consider a stone's energetic value before adding a new piece to the collection?

ABOVE Moon magic selenite pieces at London's Bamford Haybarn

"Atoms will vibrate," he says, "but that doesn't mean anything in terms of the spiritual." Rumsey takes a breath and continues, "But that doesn't mean it's not relevant, because it says a lot in terms of a placebo effect, which has a place in our culture. Rocks and stones always had a lot of power attached to them, but there is no evidence for the spiritual, or we haven't found it, yet. But like all scientists I don't rule anything out, and I'd be open-minded if anything new was proved."

Rumsey's scientific research shows that we are continually making new discoveries. Much like the internal arrangement of building-block atoms within a crystal, each piece of knowledge rests on top of another, and over hundreds of years we have built up a significant edifice of information about the world around us. The lumps of stone that Rumsey curates contain many unanswered questions, but as technology advances and knowledge improves, he thinks it's possible someone could come along in fifty years with new interpretations of the crystals in the collection.

Although this book is peppered with the names of fashion mavens, and both Jess Diner and I have written stories about crystals in the last year for British *Vogue*, I feel crystals have grown beyond temporary fashion into a movement, as people search for a new way to live amid the life-changing flux of the digital revolution and climate change. A new Stone Age has erupted from those changes.

Rumsey points out the historic importance of stones in our civilization—after all, an entire prehistoric cultural period, the Stone Age, is defined by early man's use of rocks. Exhibits in the museum illustrate the place of certain agates and flints, used as sharp tools, in our evolution as human beings. Stones became our first knives, which arguably facilitated a lot of the progress that followed. Or Rumsey says, "Take malachite, for instance. When early man took a lump of green rock and heated it over a fire, he found a copper metal inside, which he could bend and use. It must have been magical."

Rumsey speaks with authority and passion about stones and crystals, and in his scientific role at the museum, appearing the epitome of contentment, he sits surrounded by specimens and crystal in his office behind the vast Victorian galleries. Does he think working with crystals every day is beneficial for his general outlook? "No," he says with a smile. "I cycle to work each day and swim." However, Rumsey agrees that we are entering into a new Stone Age: "People are intrigued by the combination of beauty and science in crystals, and the merging of artistic features with geology, and the fact that it's been taken out of the earth." There is something about the rhythmic repetition of crystals' natural design, which appeals to the mind as well as the eye.

Since the Stone Age, humans have been picking up interesting rocks, but it was during the Renaissance that an interest was sparked in Europe to study and learn about nature.

"The driving force for this resurgence of interest in the physical world was the rise to prominence of the scholar as the third leading power in society (along with the clergy and aristocracy)."

—JOEL A. BARTSCH, WENDELL E. WILSON, AND MARK MAUTHNER, *MASTERPIECES OF THE MINERAL WORLD*

Historically, scholars relied on the support of a wealthy aristocratic patron to assemble a collection of natural objects and provide an environment for them to carry out their studies; thus the modern notion of a museum was born. Camillus Leonardus of Pesaro, Italy, author of the first mineralogical work, *Speculam Lapidum*, was the court physician to Cesare Borgia. Physicians had to be educated in the practical aspects of nature, including pharmaceutical uses of minerals and plants to treat the patron should he become ill, so the partnership of aristocrat and mineral scholar (apothecary) arguably began with a "feel better" practical purpose. During the sixteenth century, pharmaceutical collections were housed in "cabinets of curiosities," known in German as *Wunderkammer* or *Kunstkammer*, with each cabinet painted a color to harmonize with the contents inside.

Victorian watercolorist and art critic John Ruskin commented on his fascination of stones in the catalog of an 1883 mineral exhibition that he curated for St. David's School in the south of England.

> "The formation of stones is indeed a curious business. A stone can be seen [as] a mountain in miniature; and the surface of any stone is more interesting, richer in colour, more splendid in form than any ordinary hill. Nature in this way finds in a piece of stone merely two feet in diameter the chance to express all of her majestic varieties of form, and shape, and colour, and ornament, and fracture that she needs to build her great mountains."
>
> —JOHN RUSKIN, "RUMINATIONS ON THE COLLECTION OF SILICEOUS MATERIALS"

Now this age-old tradition of collecting has become a more widespread, egalitarian, and addictive pastime. Never before have so many people been involved in collecting minerals. As with anything else subject to fashion, while there are the buyers looking for vast natural "sculptures," there are always new trends. One such trend is to display unusual specimens of smaller crystals in specially built mahogany cabinets with climate control to preserve the collection, contemporary versions of the traditional cabinets of curiosities.

Stone-collecting contemporary British artist Damien Hirst created two *Wunderkammer*-style closets of semiprecious stones for his 2017 *Treasures* show in Venice; these were beautiful museum-style cabinets. He explained the inspiration to me:

> I've always loved rocks and precious stones. I started collecting them when I was six or seven—amethyst, malachite, pyrite, fool's gold. I'd seen big geodes in the Natural History Museum and loved them and wanted to possess them, fossils too. I got small ones from those little seaside shops, where you can get bits of crystal and polished bits of rose quartz and I bought a cabinet at a car boot sale to hold them all. I had a book of stones and would go through and check off the ones that I'd managed to get hold of. I used to find them on building sites, those white stones that had tiny capsules inside if you smashed them up. It felt like magic. Rocks and stamps were the first things I ever collected and it started my obsession with collecting.

Now the competition involved in this pursuit is changing the landscape of mineralogy. A new breed of art buyer is frequenting the proliferation of mineral stores and galleries featuring stones from the world's top crystal regions such as Brazil, China, and Colombia. They are creating a demand for well-formed and colored minerals, as miners are busy digging out what private collectors want to display. One blue-cap tourmaline was sold in 2011 for $1.5 million. In some cases, stones' prices can appreciate fivefold in a year. Some investment portfolios are reflecting this new pastime as connoisseurs navigate the market searching for the most exquisite crystals on Earth. The auction houses of Bonhams and Christie's, reacting to the art crowd's demands, have begun holding "Science & Natural History" sales in London and Los Angeles featuring agate slices, citrine spheres, slabs of meteorites, and malachite specimens. Some of these new collections might eventually be absorbed into museums. Others who purchase these stones aren't intending to build a vast collection. They are simply enjoying the satisfaction that comes from including a crystal or piece of sculptural geology in their home or office, or including one in their beauty-and-health regime. Including a daily gem, which has emerged from the wild chaos of nature, helps them feel free and whole.

BELOW Rock-crystal pyramid by the bedside of Sheherazade Goldsmith

Not long ago, when I traveled to Washington, DC, I spoke with Jeffrey Post, curator of the National Gem & Mineral Collection at the Smithsonian National Museum of Natural History. At the time, he contemplated adding a rough piece of yellow-green spodumene and the largest nugget of American turquoise ever found to the collection. He was also seeing the effect of the new Stone Age on those who come to the museum.

"It's harder to find ways to connect back to Earth. Visitors are flabbergasted by the minerals, and it gives them a whole different sense of Earth, science, and themselves. What's the point of these exhibits unless we change people?" he explains. "Minerals are the most effective change agent in the museum. Real objects open up curiosity, awe, and learning. We put the third dimension back into the minds of people who are bored of pictures on Instagram. Our mission is to help inform about the world we are living in, and to use the information gained to make better decisions."

Back in the world of fashion, I bumped into Elaine Sullivan of the Tod's Group, who swaps her crystal necklace for amethyst, or sometimes a small ruby, depending on what's happening in her life. "It helps to change my state of mind," she tells me. "The energy is inside me, but the crystals open it up; call it whatever you want, but it's a positive thing." Model and environmental campaigner Arizona Muse has left her new baby daughter at home with a gift of rose quartz in the corner of her crib. "If people don't respect crystals," she declares, "it's probably because they haven't encountered them." Arizona is a champion for sustainable behavior, particularly in the world of fast fashion where she believes change is urgently needed. *Buy better, buy less* is her motto. A crystal is with us for our lifetime—and then who knows how many lifetimes beyond.

To me that's the definition of something precious. For others it could be rare diamonds set into a piece of dazzling jewelry, or in this overcrowded world, some highly prize a larger space, while others hanker after a new Damien Hirst to fill the space on a white wall. The stones in Hirst's *Treasures* show were included alongside the cabinets of coins and ingots—one naturally occurring and one man-made.

"Both were about ideas of value, though, and how we place it on certain things and how it shifts and changes over time," explains Hirst. "A precious stone, unlike a certain shape of coin, is always going to have value and allure, though, because of its inherent beauty; humans can't resist it." When that beauty can also spark a process of joy or transformation in our life, then it's invested with a culture beyond value. Indeed, a change agent that propels a leaden state of mind to realize its own potential, kindling a more joyful way to live, could be viewed as priceless.

Of course, there's also the future to worry about, which doesn't look too bright; environmental concerns combined with political instability and exhaustion from the rat race have made stress and depression global health emergencies. A crystal can pull you through the darkness and become the instrument of a life well spent. Ego block can be penetrated by these colored fragments and you can access a broader understanding of your own domain of feelings, thoughts, and actions as well as the wider world. As Ghandi pointed out, "If we could change ourselves, the tendencies in the world would also change. . . ." As we face the future in this age of upheaval, it's comforting to look for something familiar from the past. Stones, rocks, crystals—call them what you will—lend us an encouraging sense of solidity and strength.

I think about the girl with the bead necklace and speculate that her family might have had an ochre painting kit to mark their bodies. It wasn't long before early *Homo sapiens* added a type of hematite stone, scratched from molten rock, to the earthy mixture, as the reflective metal flakes would have made the paint glitter. That must have appeared like magic. Interestingly, after a session with Emma Lucy Knowles, she recommended that I use hematite. "Not for everyday use," she impresses, but "for grounding after a challenging day or overly creative day that leaves you feeling a little drunk on the energy." Completing a book sounds like the ideal hematite moment.

We share with our ancestors a breathtaking attraction to pistachio-colored jade, carbuncle of fiery red, chunk of rose-pink quartz, or the fragment of a rainbow gleaming from an olive-green labradorite, or the pearly whiteness of the moonstone. These stones, combined with a mystical antiquity, lend us the calming resources they've carried with them from beneath the earth, where they were formed in dark mountain caverns. Use them, and your inner life will lead your outer self to a new way of being.

Stones can alter minds, open hearts, and help us understand our place in relation to the natural world. When life is uncomfortable, the simple knowledge that you are in possession of a unique fragment of nature, with a heart-melting color vibrating with an ancient history from the earth's depths, can almost feel like magic.

Acknowledgments

It could be the crystal effect but many people have supported this book. The experience has been overwhelming in positivity, collaboration, and inclusivity. I need to thank everyone involved in the book for their unfailing good nature as we disturbed homes and rifled through personal collections to shoot stones in situ. Without their help, the book would not exist.

I am so grateful to Robert Procop, my host at the Tucson Gem Fair, for opening his amazing crystal Sunset Boulevard home to me, to Peter Adler for his generosity and hospitality at his Pebble London treasure trove, and Dale Rogers for letting me loose among his mineral specimen collection and crystal-laden home.

Also, I'm in indebted to the wonderful women who shared their stories with me, as well as photographer Jon Day, with the assistance of Russell Duncan, for their hard work bringing the stones to life.

The team at Ten Speed Press, led by Kelly Snowden and including Kimmy Tejasindhu, Emma Campion, Lisa Bieser, Leona Legarte, Dan Myers, and Jane Chinn, have my thanks for both their efficiency and creativity in bringing the book to fruition, and my agent Kirsten Neuhaus for immediately seeing the possibilities when I visited her in New York and first voiced the idea.

And last, first, and everything in between, to my family for their unfailing love and support for my jeweled enthusiasms.

OPPOSITE Statement turquoise jewelry created in bronze by Lisa Eisner and pictured on a granite stone in her Los Angeles home

About the Author

CAROL WOOLTON is a jewelry historian, editor, stylist, and jewelry editor of British *Vogue* for twenty years, where she remains as contributing jewelry director. She was the first jewelry editor of *Tatler* magazine and has contributed to multiple newspapers, magazines, and online supplements around the world, including the *Financial Times*, *Vanity Fair*, *Air Mail*, the *Daily Telegraph*, and American *Vogue*. She curates jewelry exhibitions and *The New Stone Age* is her fifth book on the subject.

She currently lives in London, where she co-founded The Leopards Jewelry Awards as a charitable initiative to support heritage crafts and skills, as well as mentor young people into the jewelry industry.

OPPOSITE Amethyst geode making a water feature in the garden of Dale Rogers

Index

Published in the United States by Ten Speed Press, an imprint of
Random House, a division of Penguin Random House LLC, New York.
www.tenspeed.com

Ten Speed Press and the Ten Speed Press colophon are registered
trademarks of Penguin Random House LLC.

Library of Congress Cataloging-in-Publication Data
  Names: Woolton, Carol, author.
  Title: The New Stone Age: ideas and inspiration for living with
    crystals / by Carol Woolton.
  Description: Regular. | Emeryville, California: Ten Speed Press, 2020.
    | Includes bibliographical references and index.
  Identifiers: LCCN 2019030973 | ISBN 9781984856593 (hardcover) |
    ISBN 9781984856609 (epub)
  Subjects: LCSH: Crystals—Miscellanea
  Classification: LCC BF1442.C78 W66 2020 | DDC 133/.2548—dc23
    LC record available at https://lccn.loc.gov/2019030973

Hardcover ISBN: 978-1-9848-5659-3
eBook ISBN: 978-1-9848-5660-9

Printed in China

Design by Lisa Bieser and Leona Legarte

10 9 8 7 6 5 4 3 2 1

First Edition